Butterflies Original Prints
Mother Earth Series

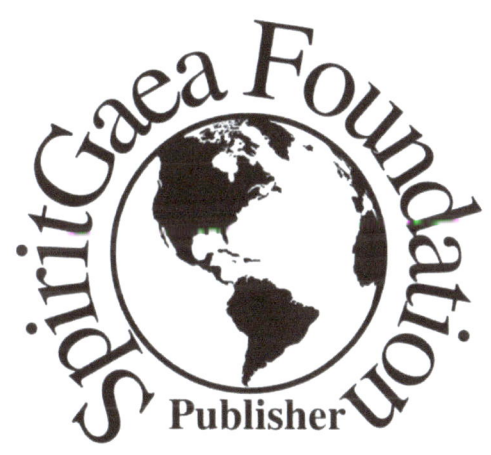
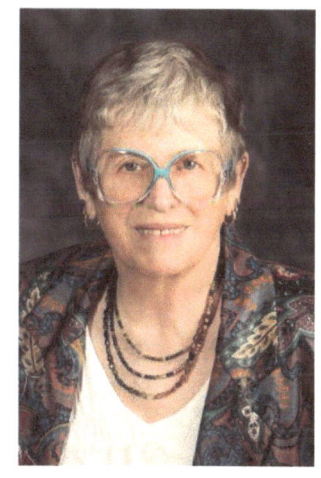

Author Artist **Jeri Lee C.Ht.**

Copyright Jerilee.com
2022
All rights Reserved

ISBN: 9798388234476

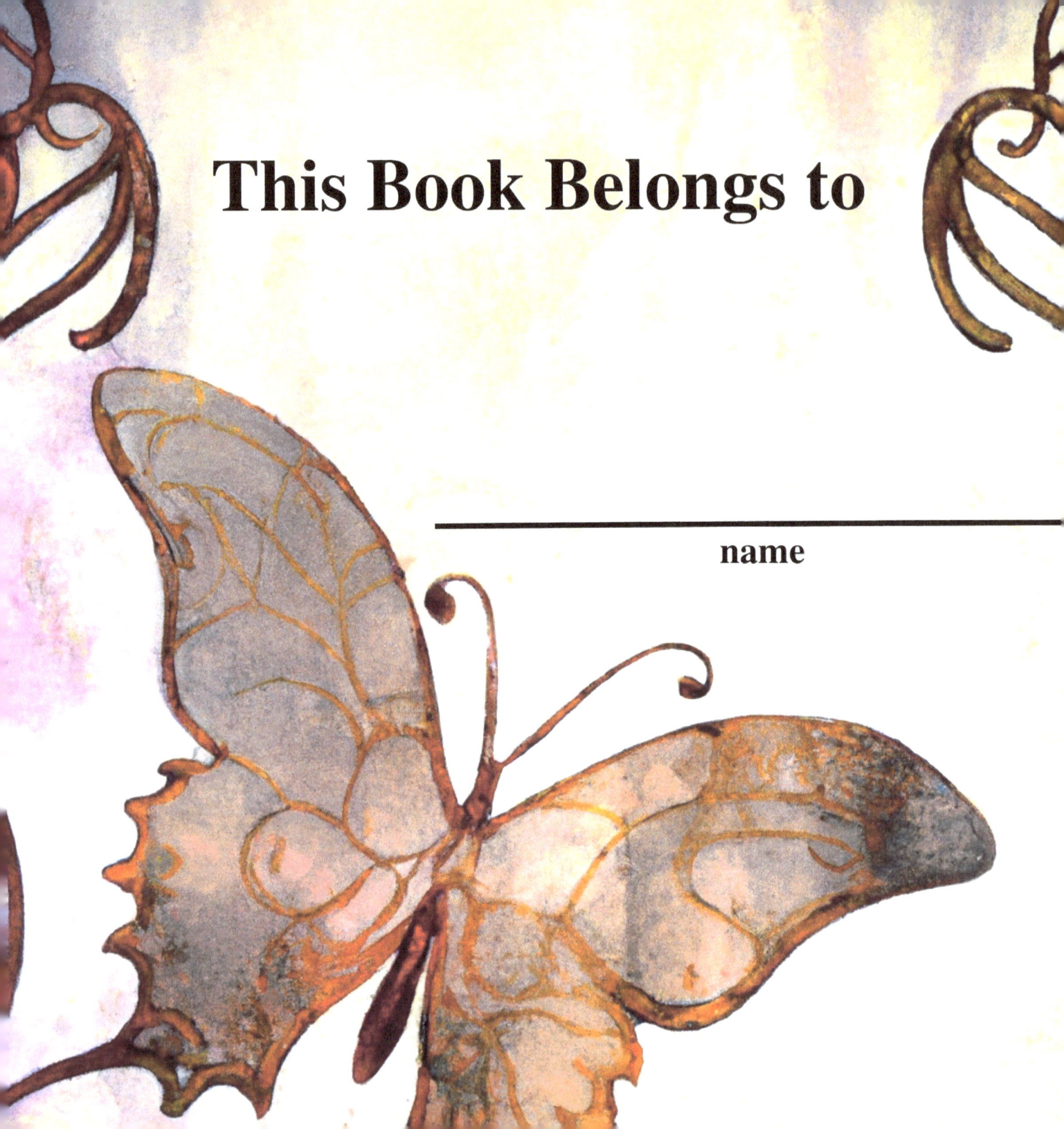

Butterflies

This book of prints is perfect for anyone looking to for beautiful artwork of unique butterflies to decorate your walls.

Butterflies are essential pollinators, meaning they transfer pollen from one flower to another while they feed on nectar. This helps flowers and plants reproduce, providing food for other animals. Additionally, butterflies provide a vital link in the food chain as both predators and prey. Predators such as birds, reptiles and spiders rely on butterflies for their diet while other insects use them as food sources. Finally, some species of butterfly help disperse seeds over long distances which can be essential for the survival of certain plant species.

The average lifestyle of a butterfly consists of four stages: egg, larva (caterpillar), pupa (chrysalis), and adult. During the egg stage, female butterflies lay their eggs on the leaves or stems of host plants. During the caterpillar stage, the larvae constantly feed to grow and molt several times before forming a chrysalis. In the pupal stage, they undergo metamorphosis into an adult butterflies by breaking down all existing tissue and reconstructing it as wings and other body parts. Finally, in adulthood, butterflies feed on nectar from flowers while also engaging in courtship behaviors to reproduce.

To reflect and refract light from the tiny scales on their wings. These scales are pigmented with various colors, including blues, greens, yellows, oranges, and reds. When the light hits these tiny structures, it is reflected in numerous hues, creating their beautiful display of color.

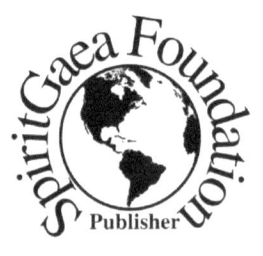

Author Artist

**Original Art
by Jeri Lee**

Copyright Jerilee.com
2022
All rights Reserved

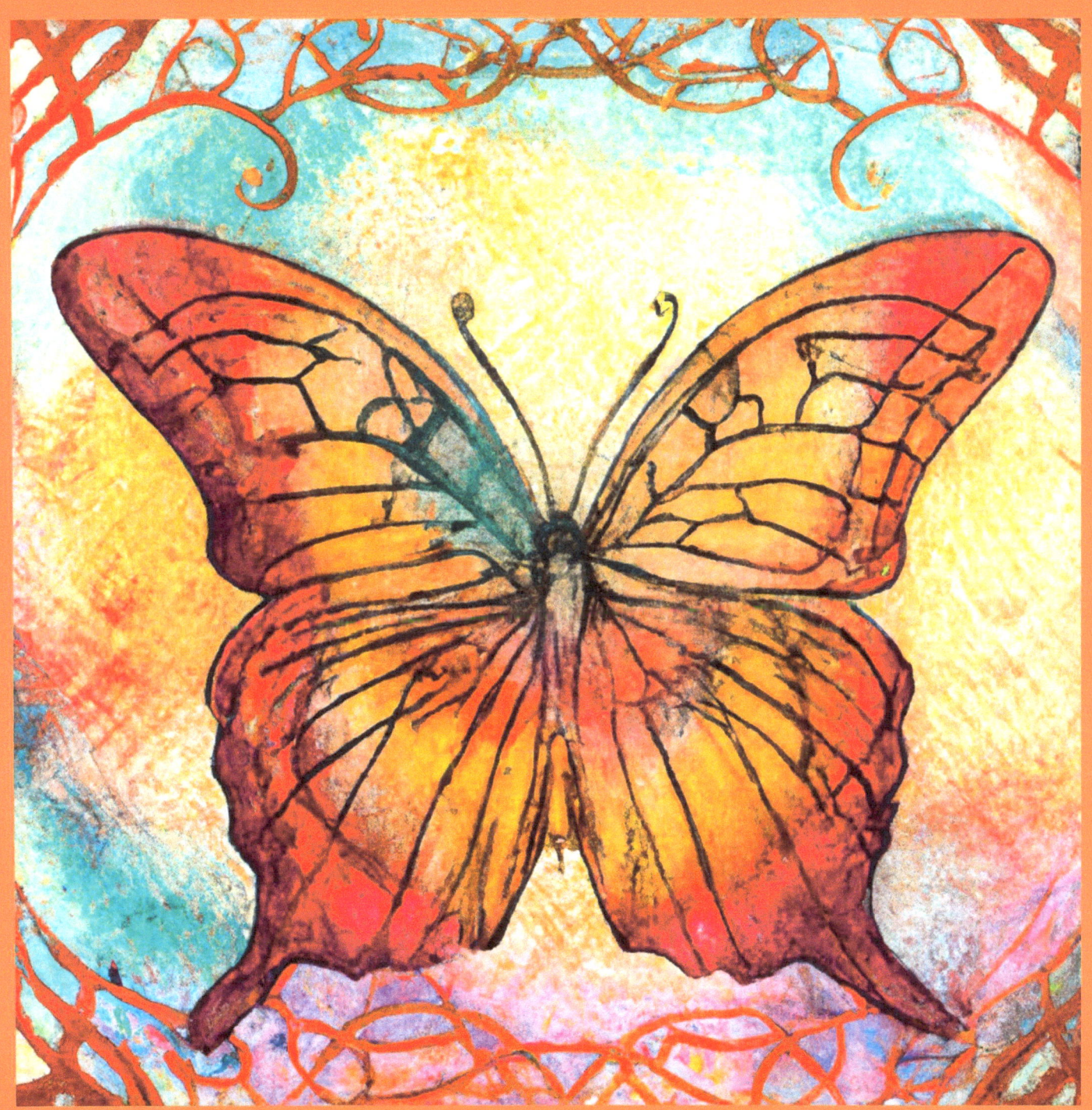

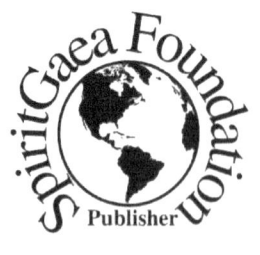

Author Artist

**Original Art
by Jeri Lee**

Copyright Jerilee.com
2022
All rights Reserved

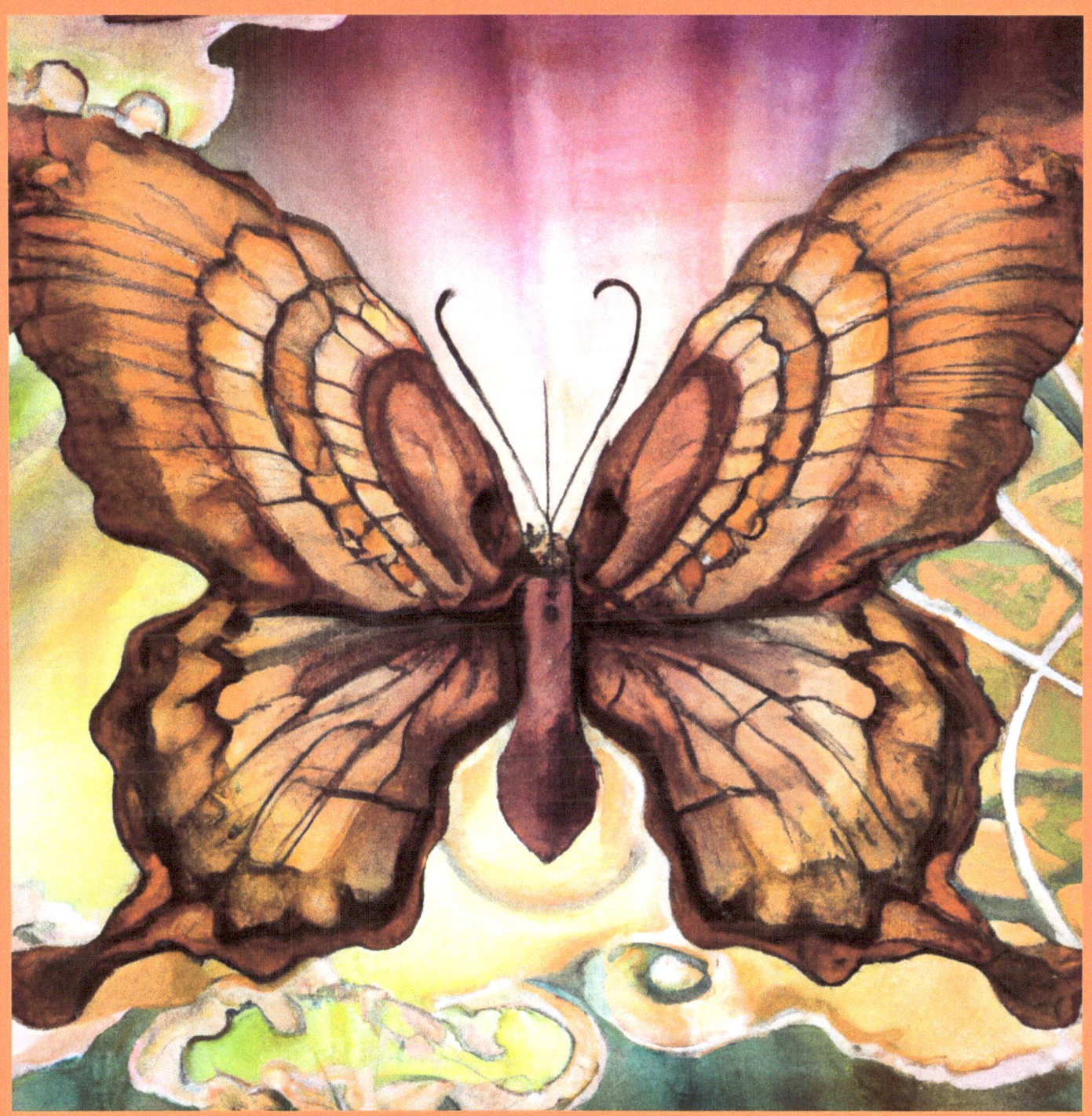

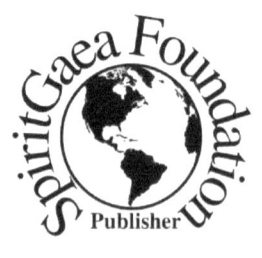

Author Artist

**Original Art
by Jeri Lee**

Copyright Jerilee.com
2022
All rights Reserved

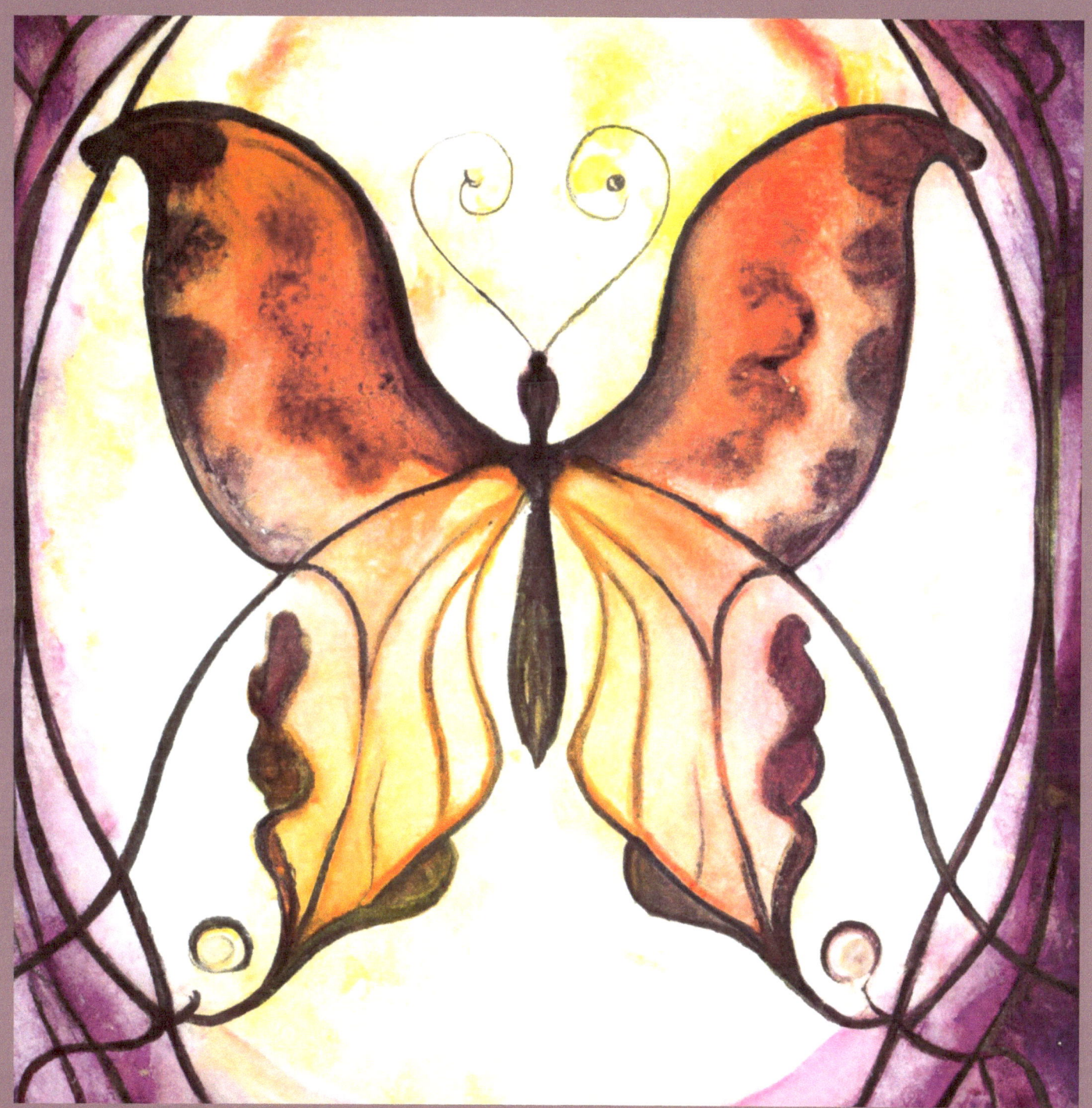

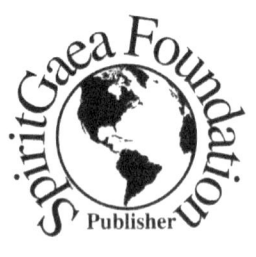

Author Artist

**Original Art
by Jeri Lee**

Copyright Jerilee.com
2022
All rights Reserved

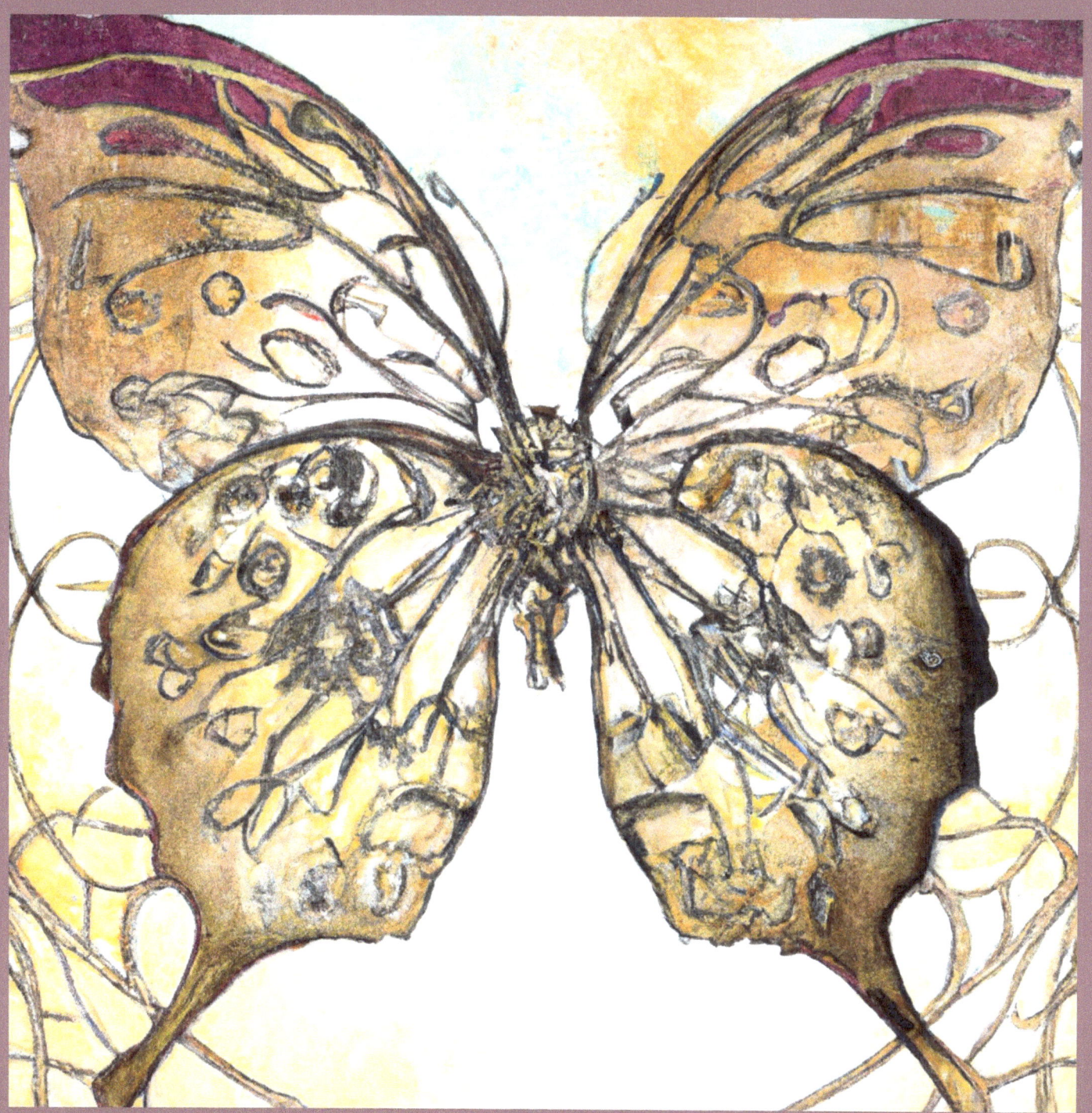

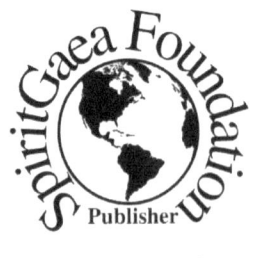

**Original Art
by Jeri Lee**

Copyright Jerilee.com
2022
All rights Reserved

Author Artist

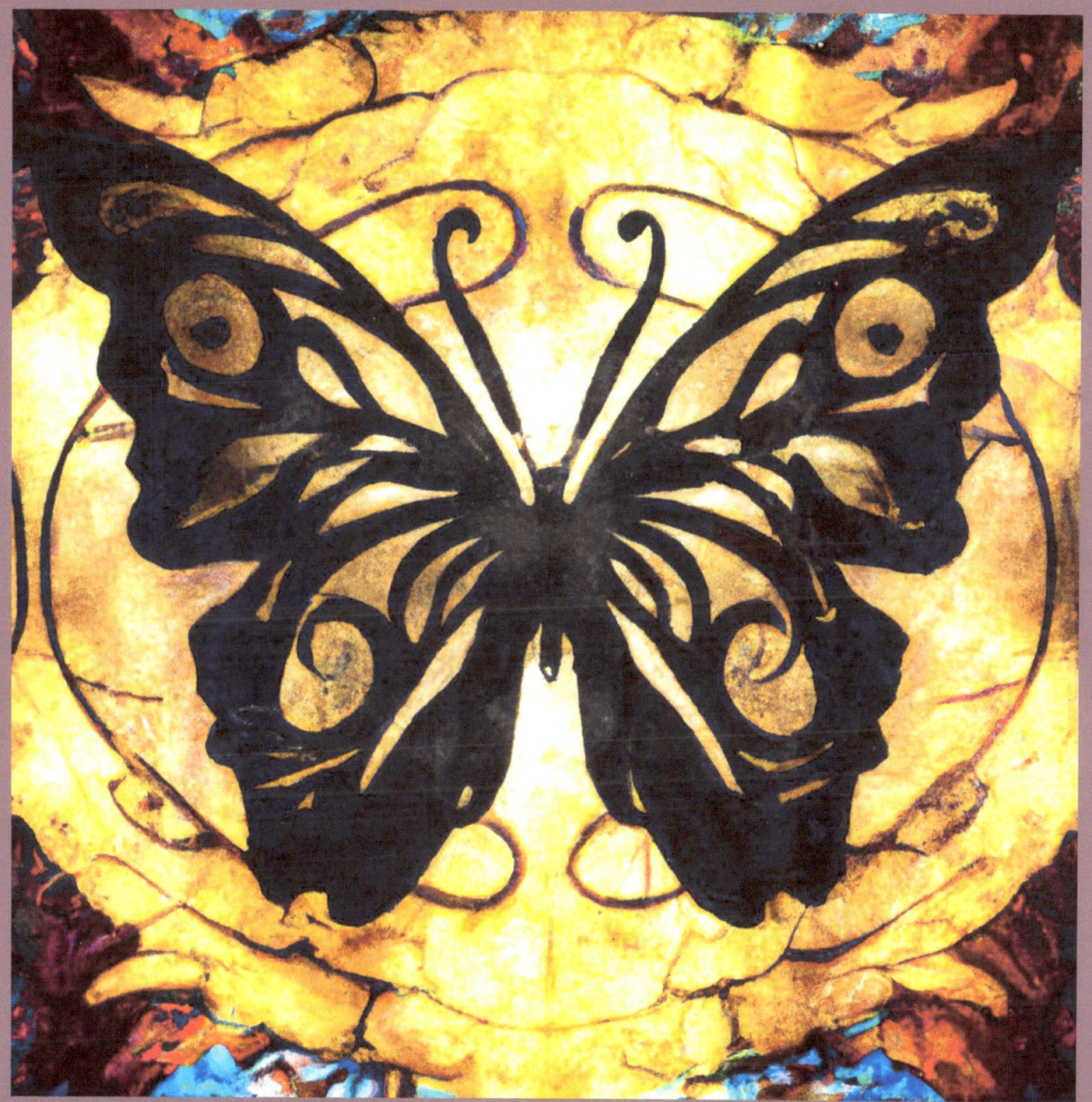

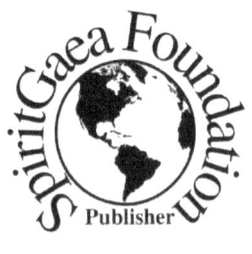

Author Artist

**Original Art
by Jeri Lee**

Copyright Jerilee.com
2022
All rights Reserved

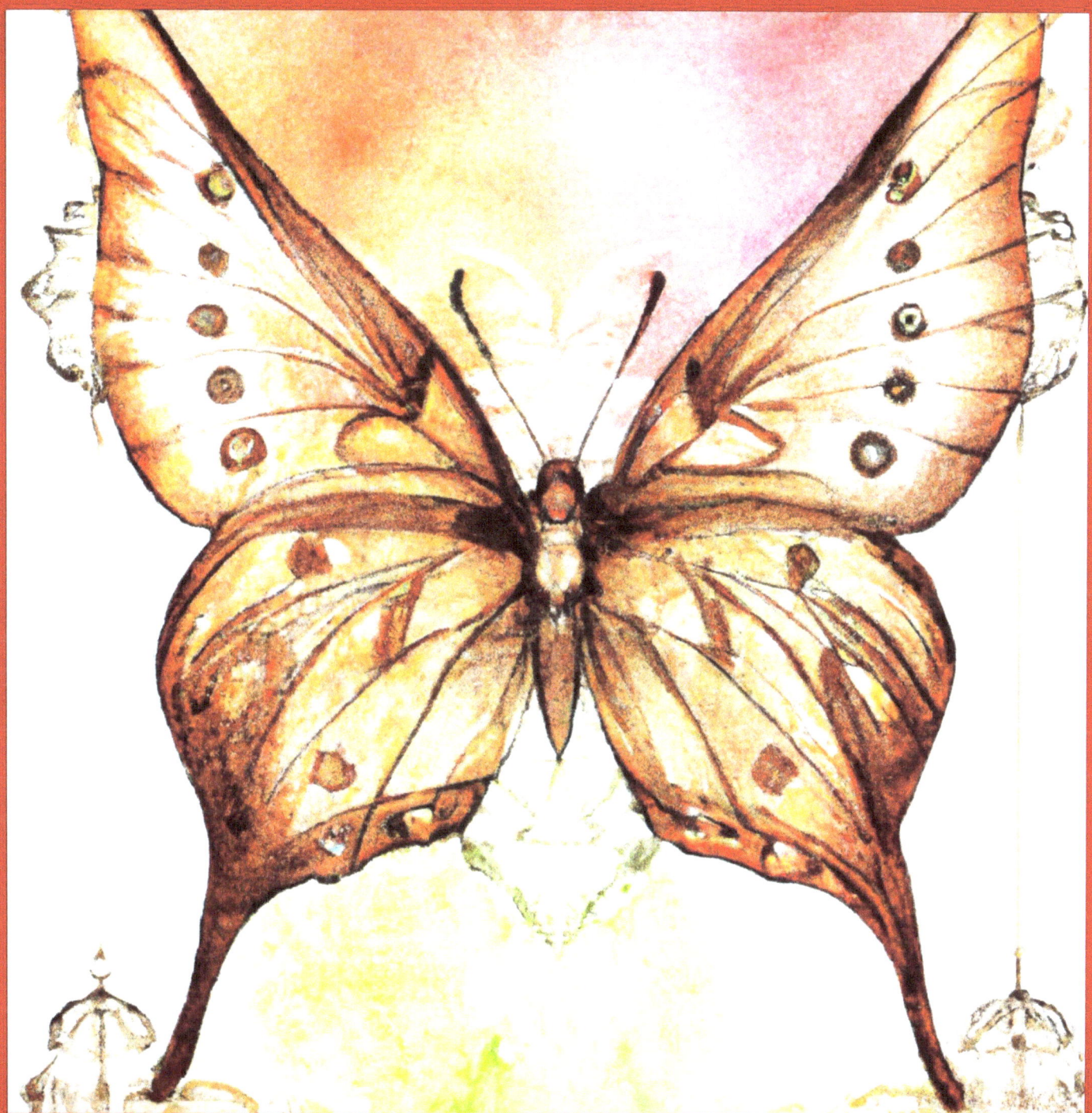

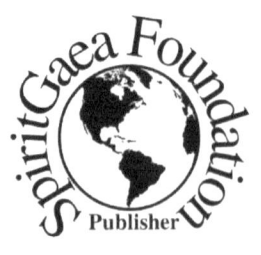

Author Artist

**Original Art
by Jeri Lee**

Copyright Jerilee.com
2022
All rights Reserved

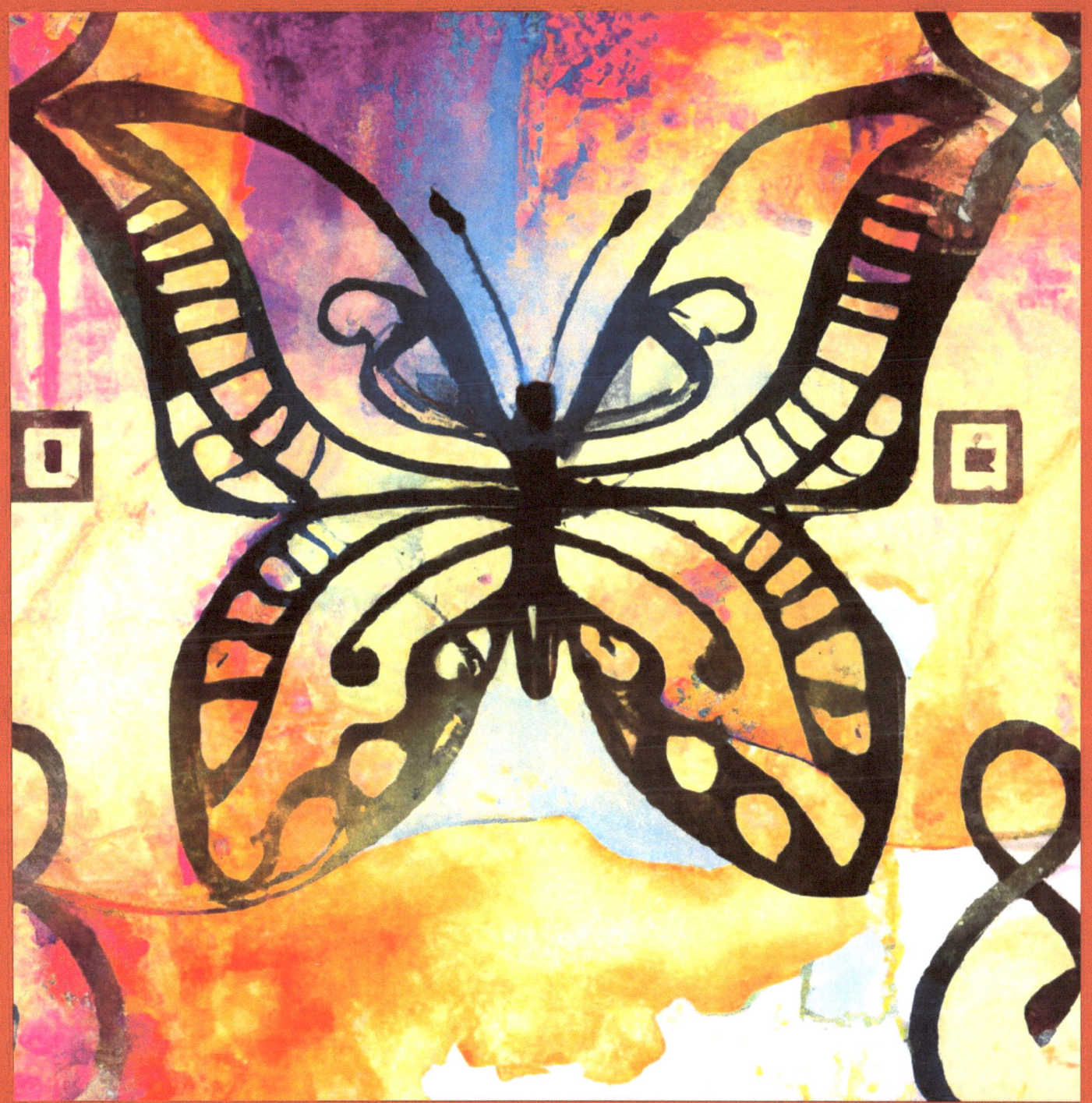

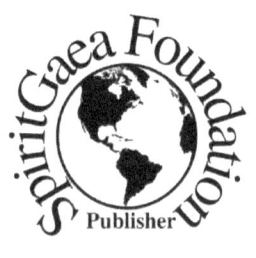

Author Artist

**Original Art
by Jeri Lee**

Copyright Jerilee.com
2022
All rights Reserved

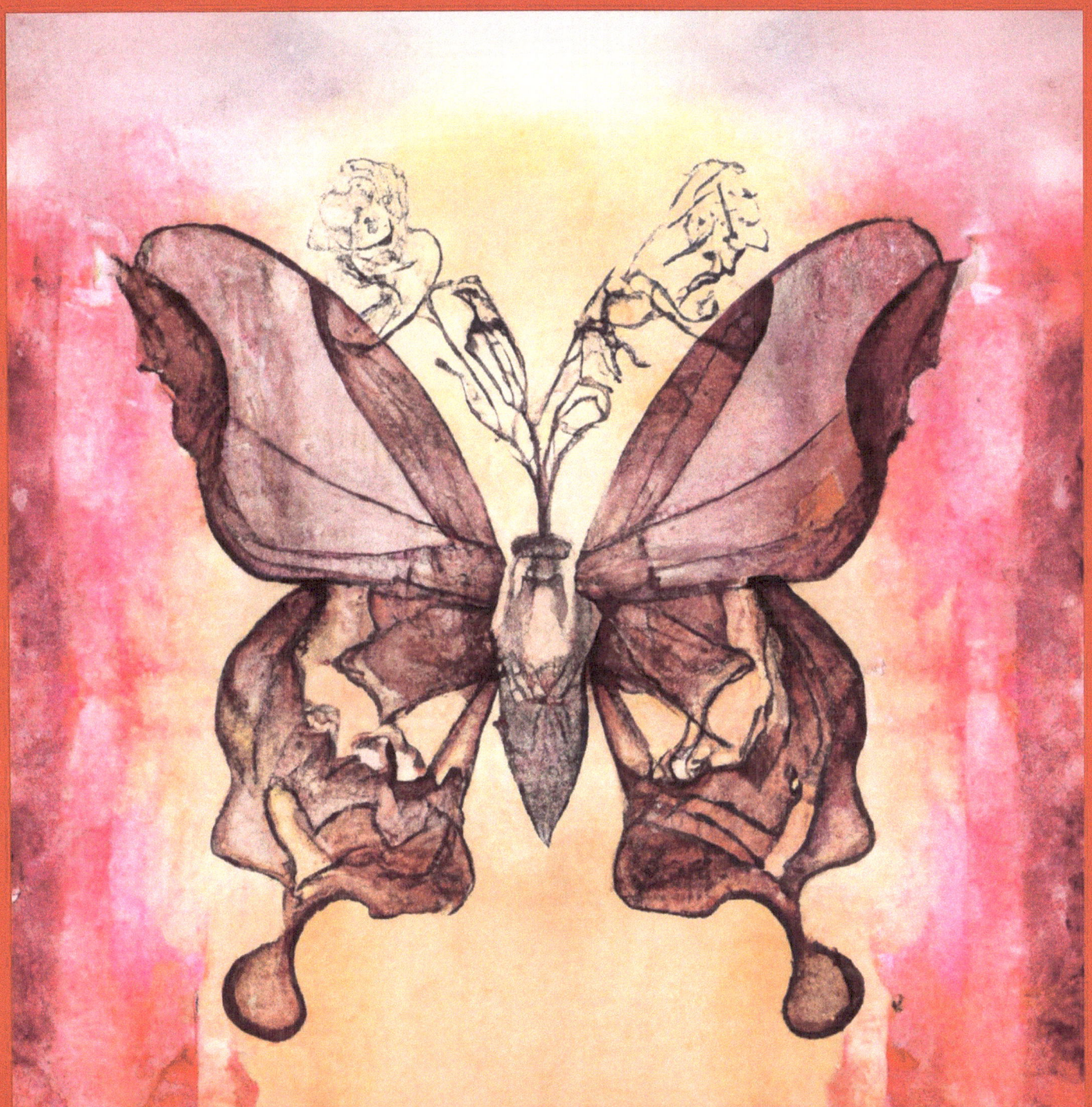

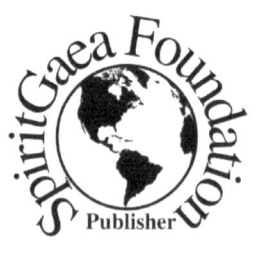

Author Artist

**Original Art
by Jeri Lee**

Copyright Jerilee.com
2022
All rights Reserved

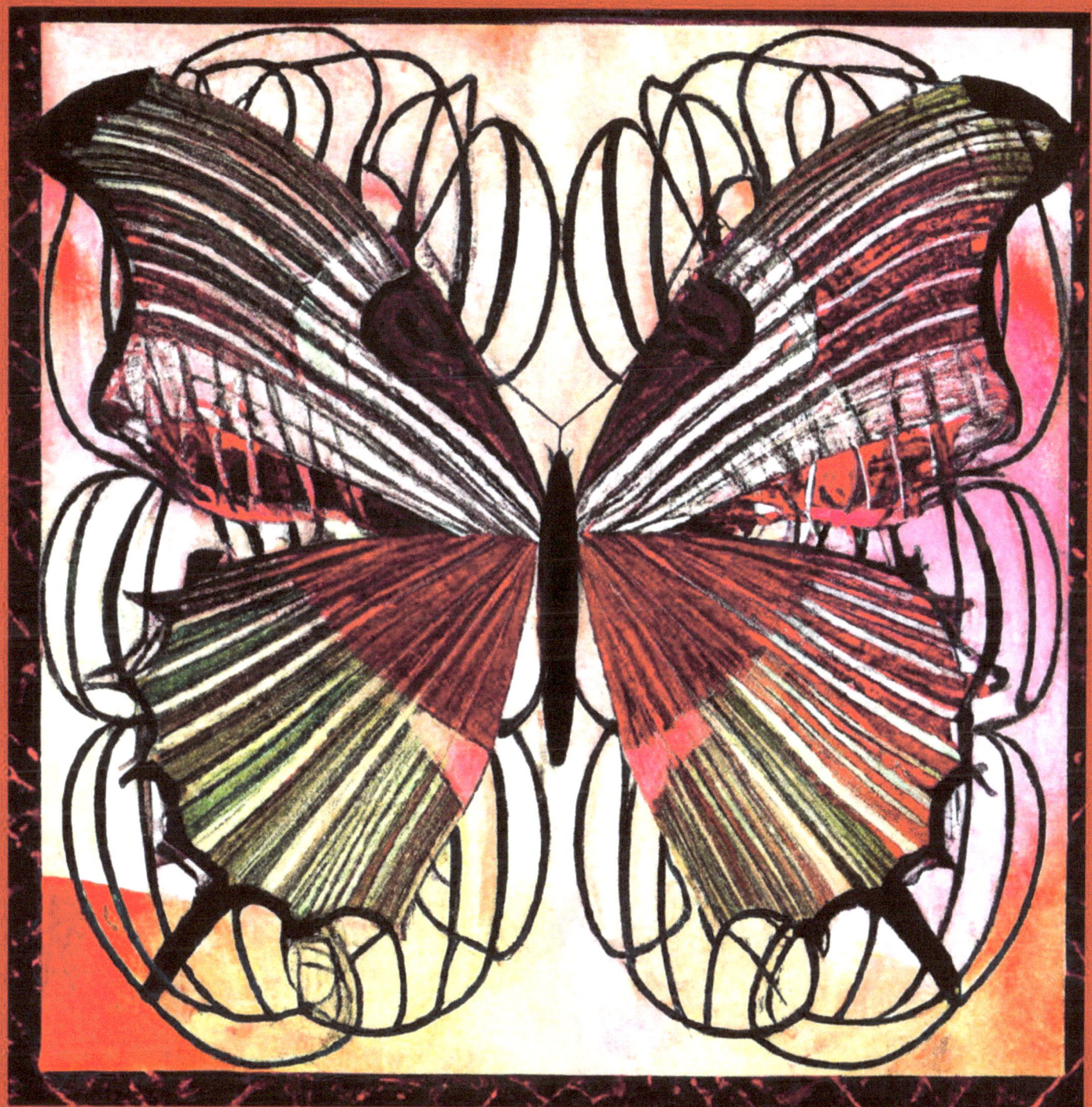

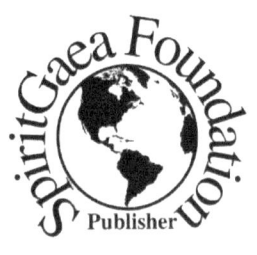

Author Artist

**Original Art
by Jeri Lee**

Copyright Jerilee.com
2022
All rights Reserved

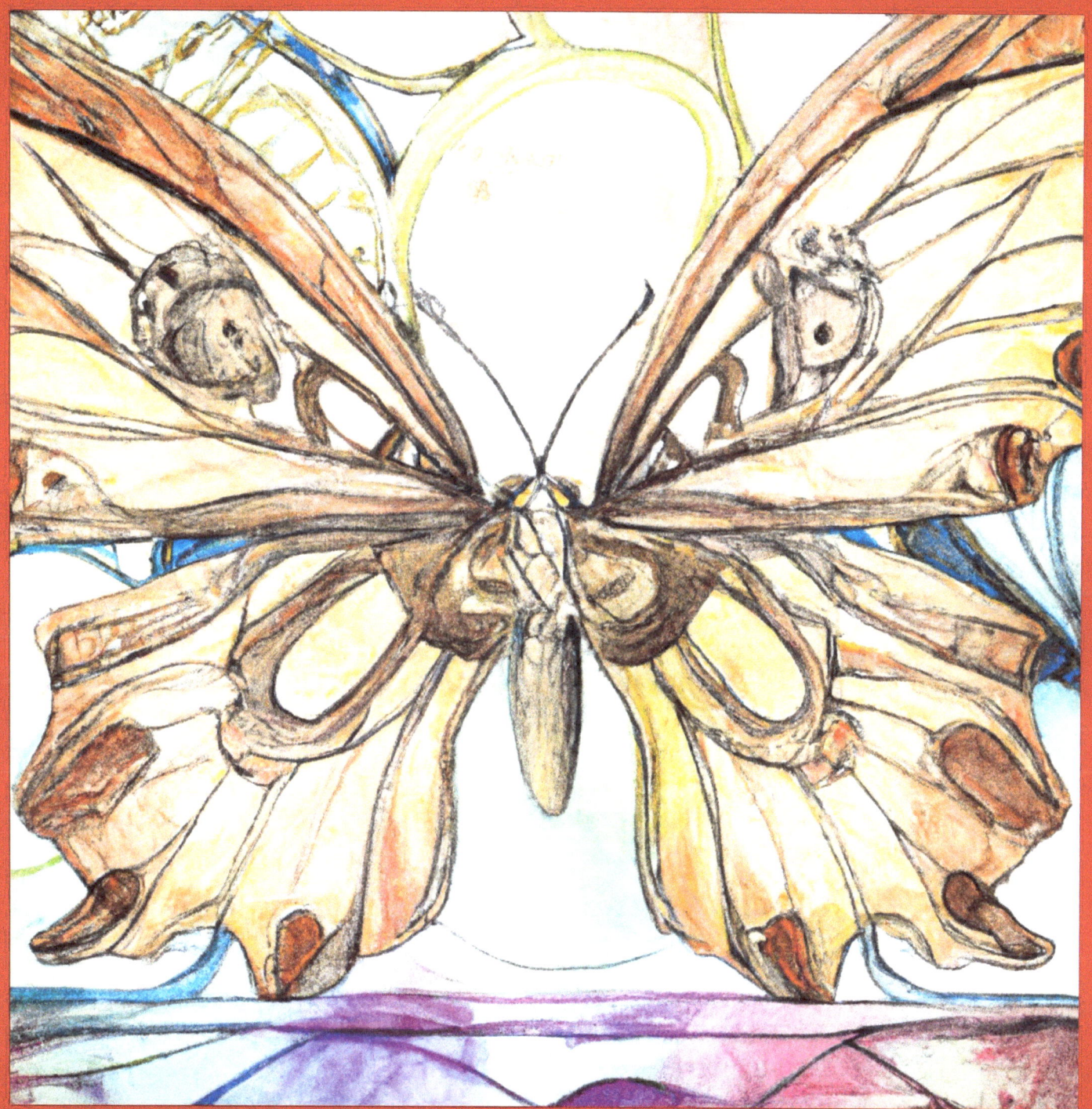

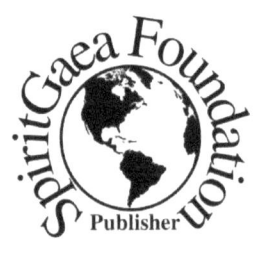

Author Artist

**Original Art
by Jeri Lee**

Copyright Jerilee.com
2022
All rights Reserved

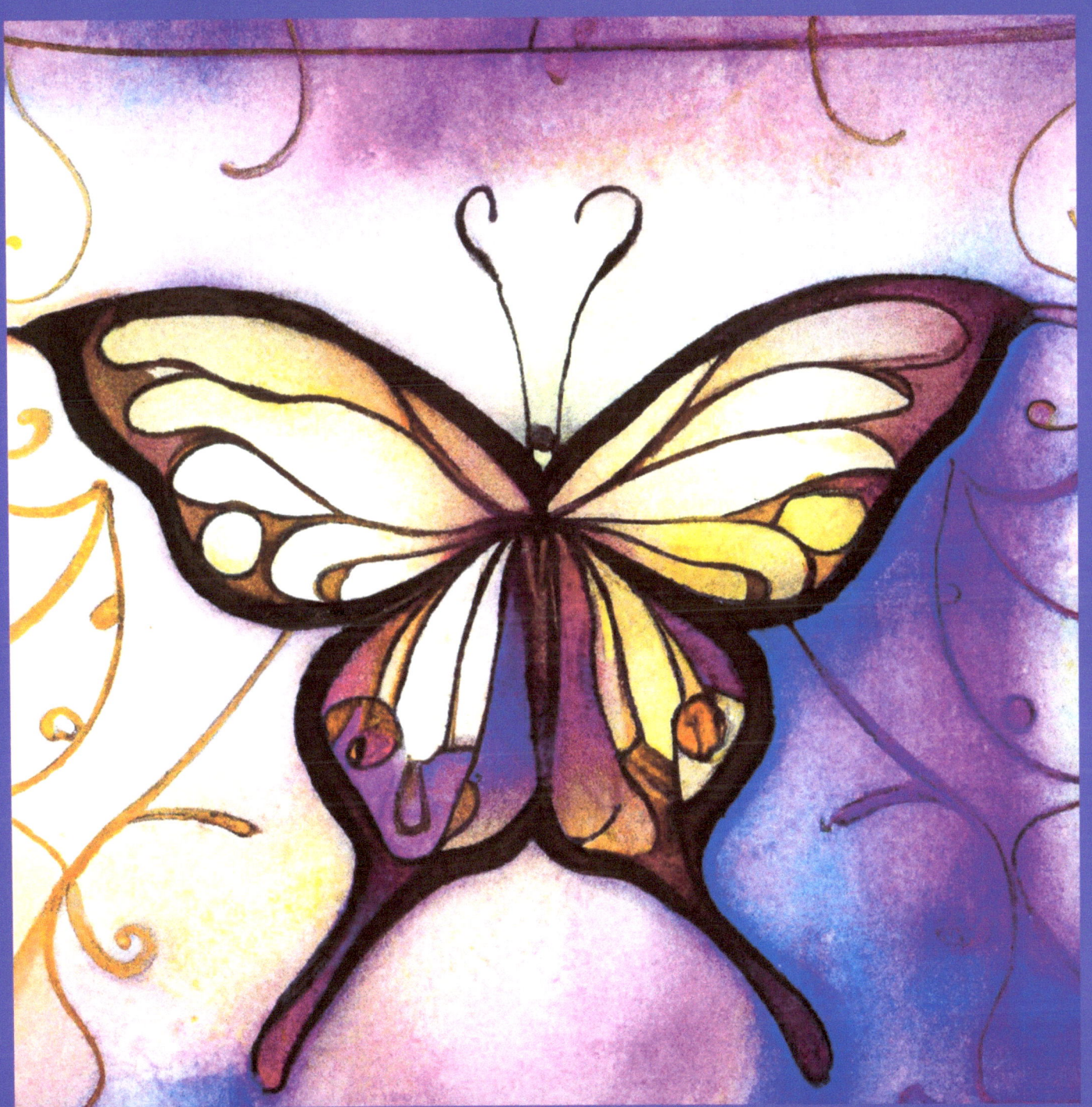

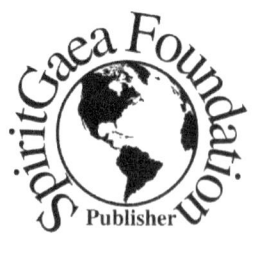

Author Artist

**Original Art
by Jeri Lee**

Copyright Jerilee.com
2022
All rights Reserved

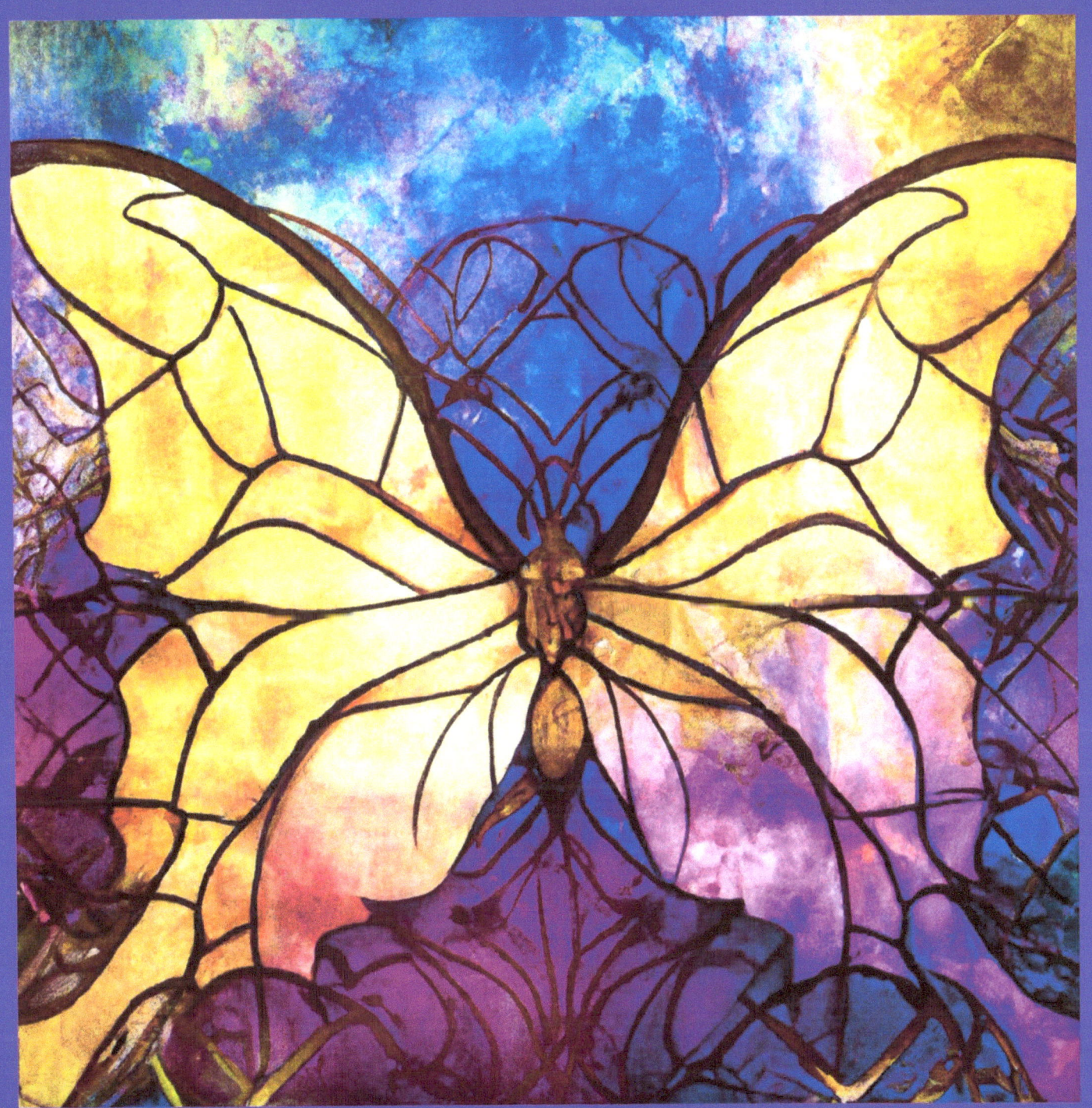

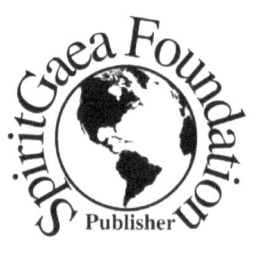

Author Artist

**Original Art
by Jeri Lee**

Copyright Jerilee.com
2022
All rights Reserved

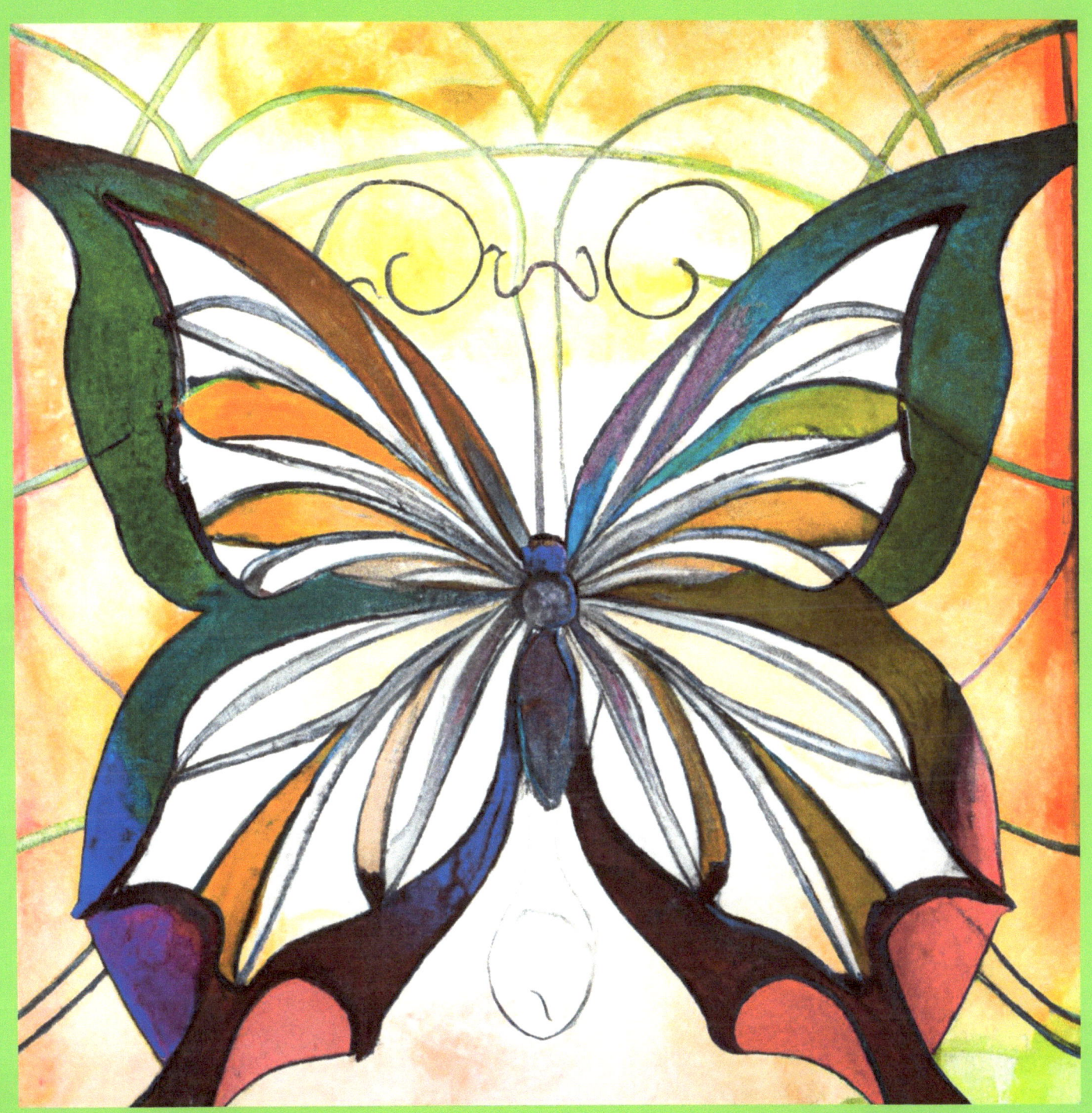

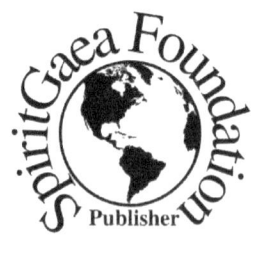

Author Artist

**Original Art
by Jeri Lee**

Copyright Jerilee.com
2022
All rights Reserved

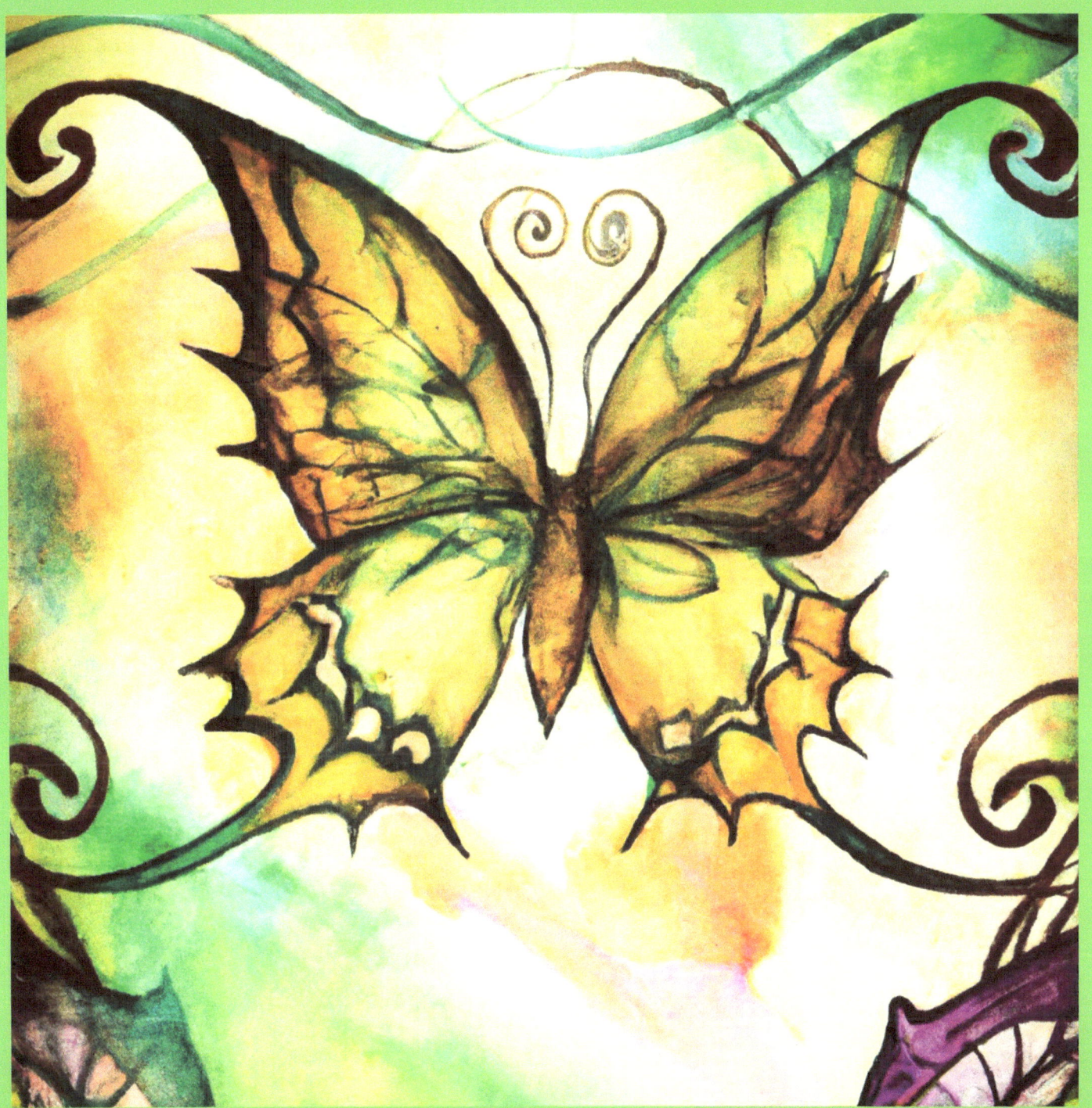

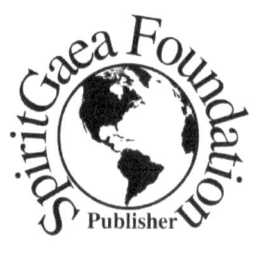

Original Art by Jeri Lee

Copyright Jerilee.com
2022
All rights Reserved

Author Artist

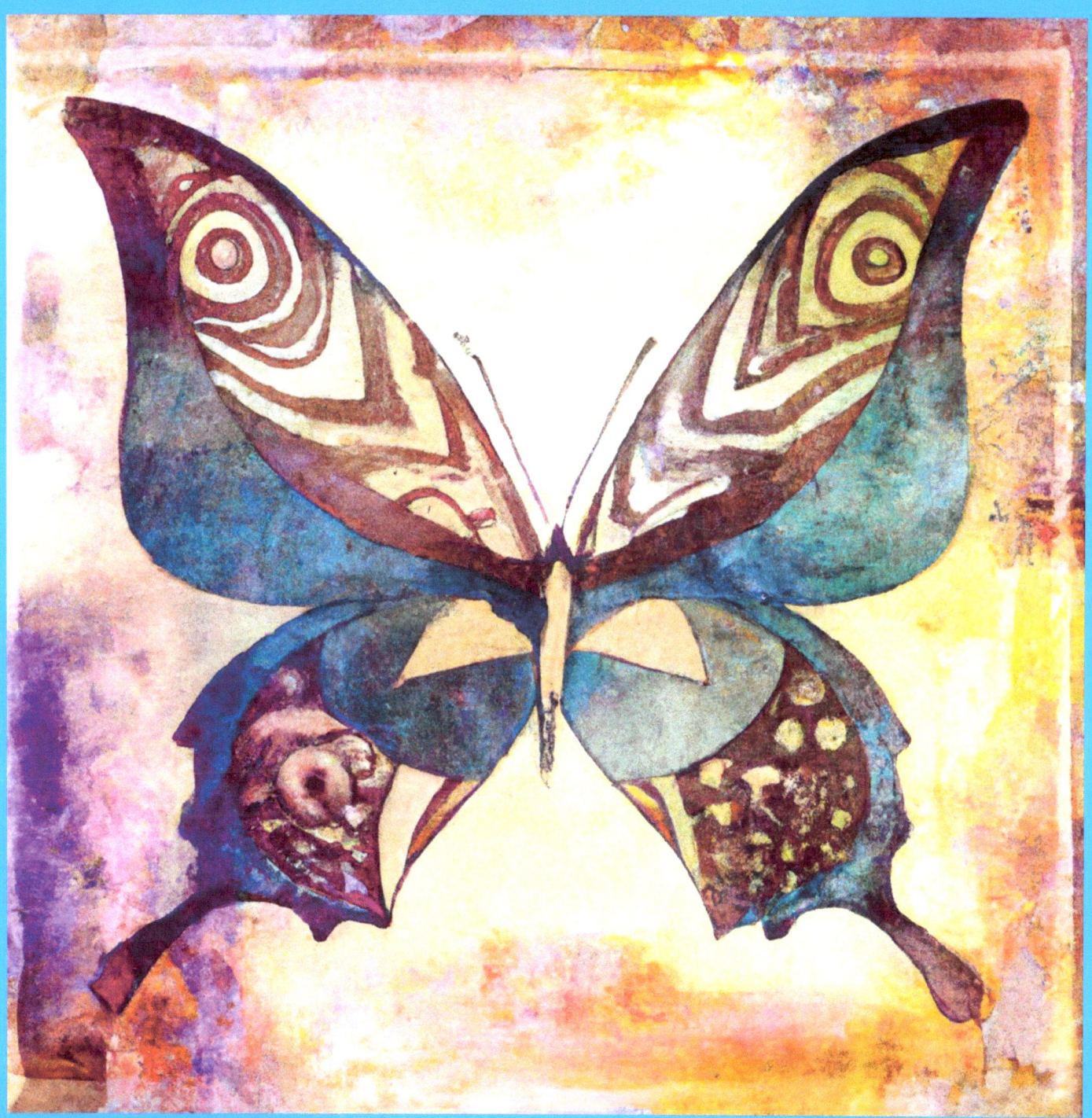

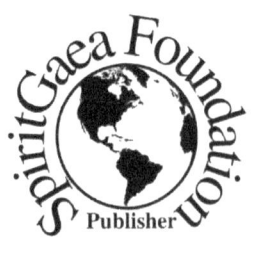

**Original Art
by Jeri Lee**

Copyright Jerilee.com
2022
All rights Reserved

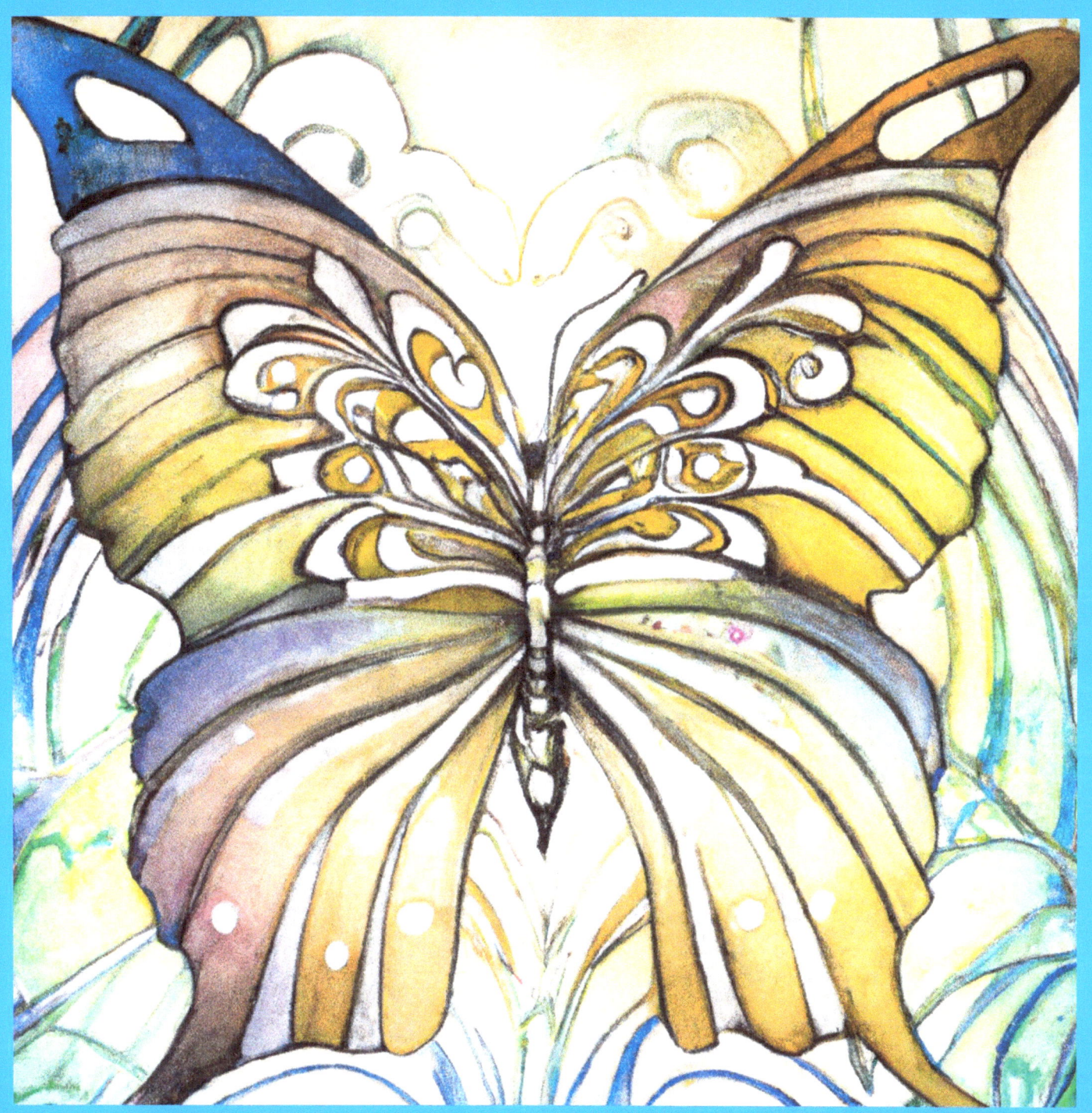

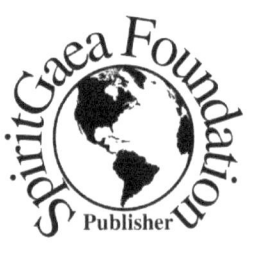

Author Artist

**Original Art
by Jeri Lee**

Copyright Jerilee.com
2022
All rights Reserved

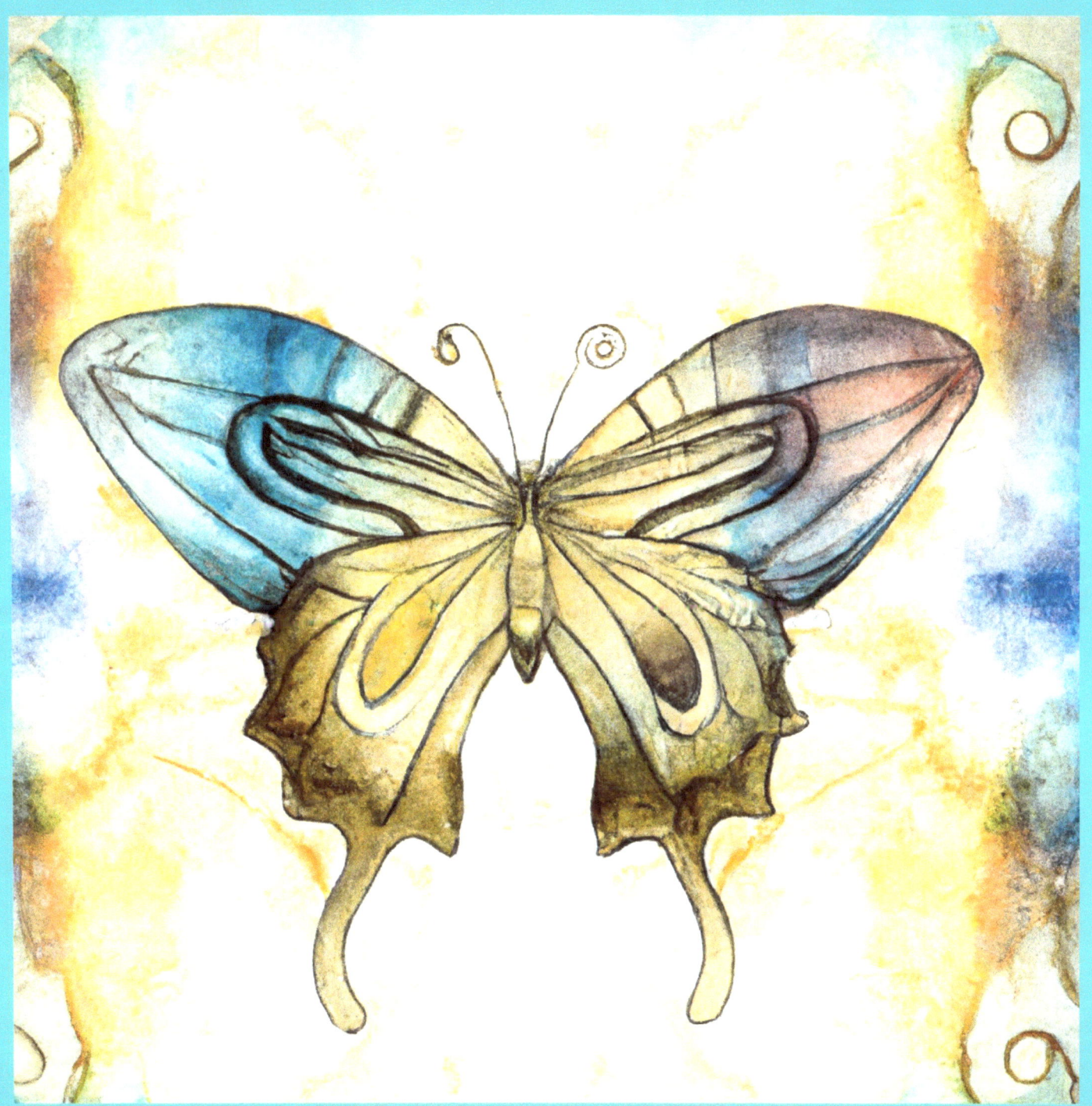

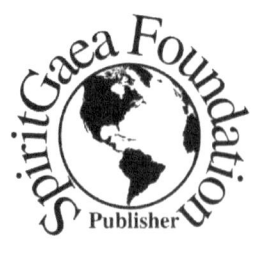

Author Artist

**Original Art
by Jeri Lee**

Copyright Jerilee.com
2022
All rights Reserved

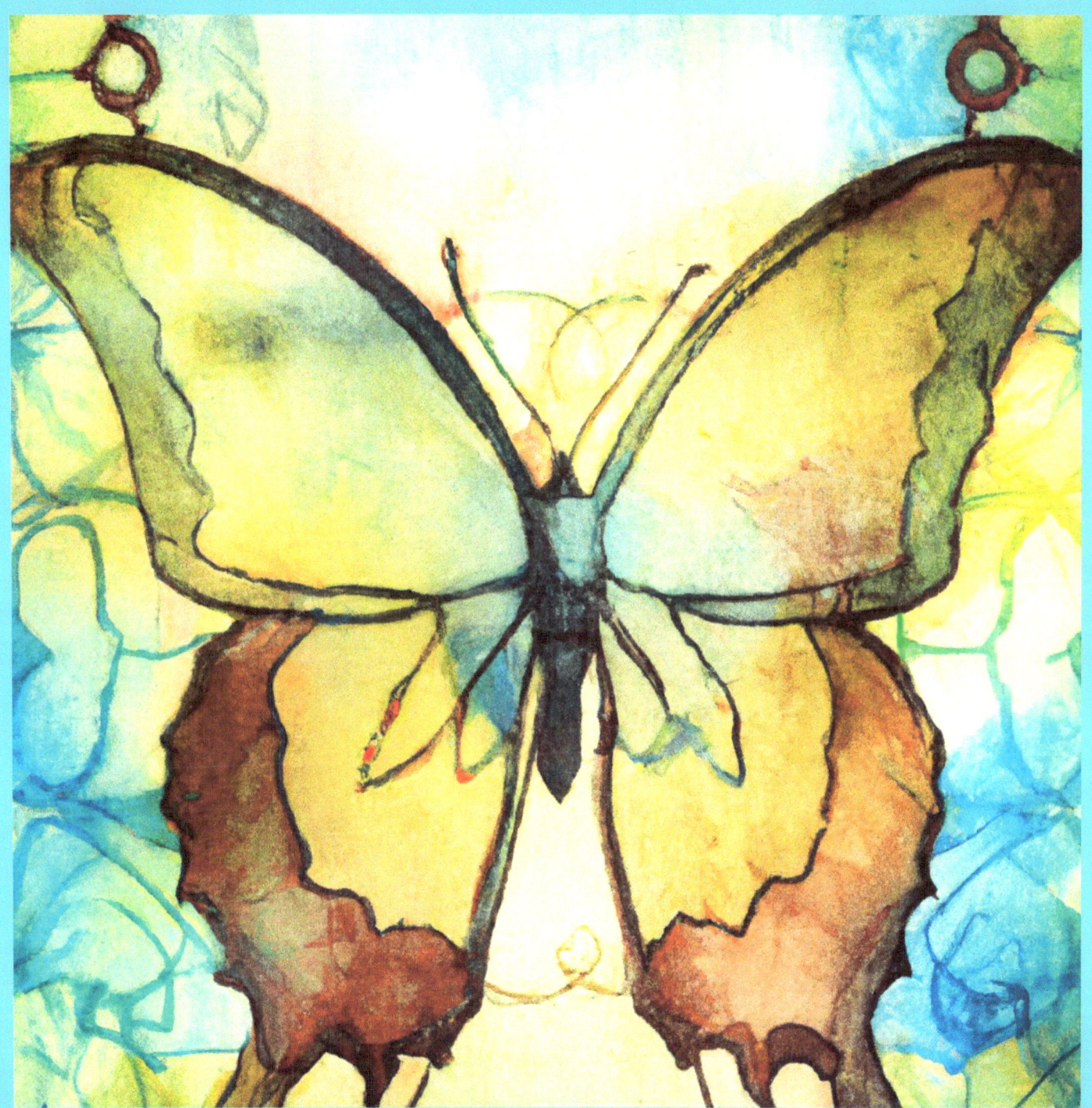

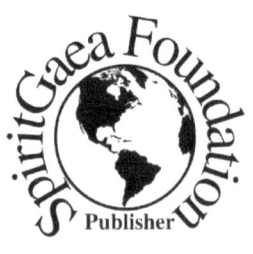

Author Artist

**Original Art
by Jeri Lee**

Copyright Jerilee.com
2022
All rights Reserved

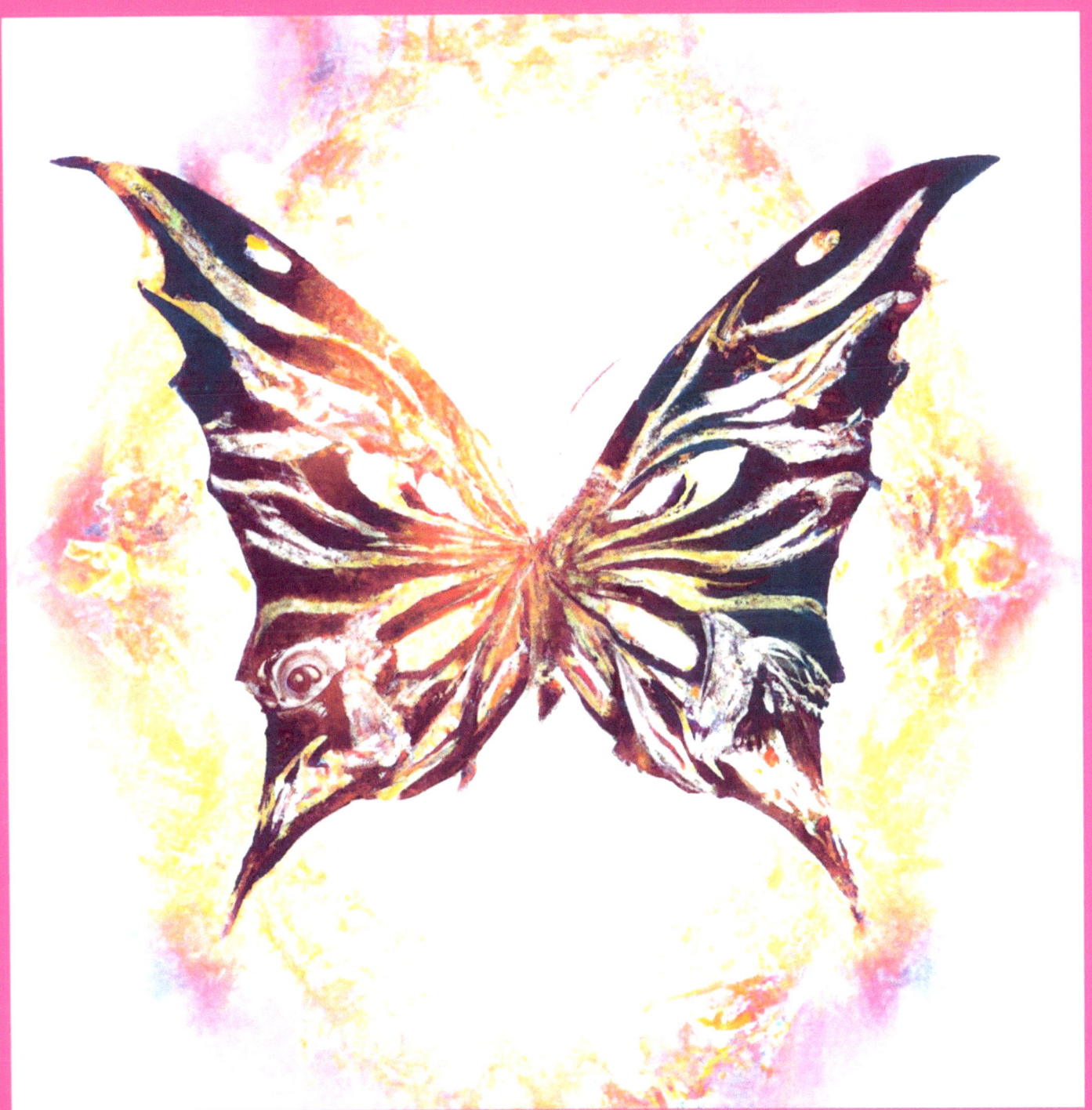

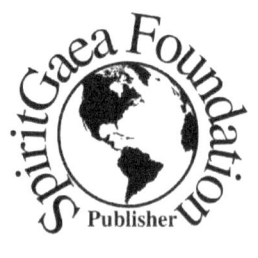

Author Artist

**Original Art
by Jeri Lee**

Copyright Jerilee.com
2022
All rights Reserved

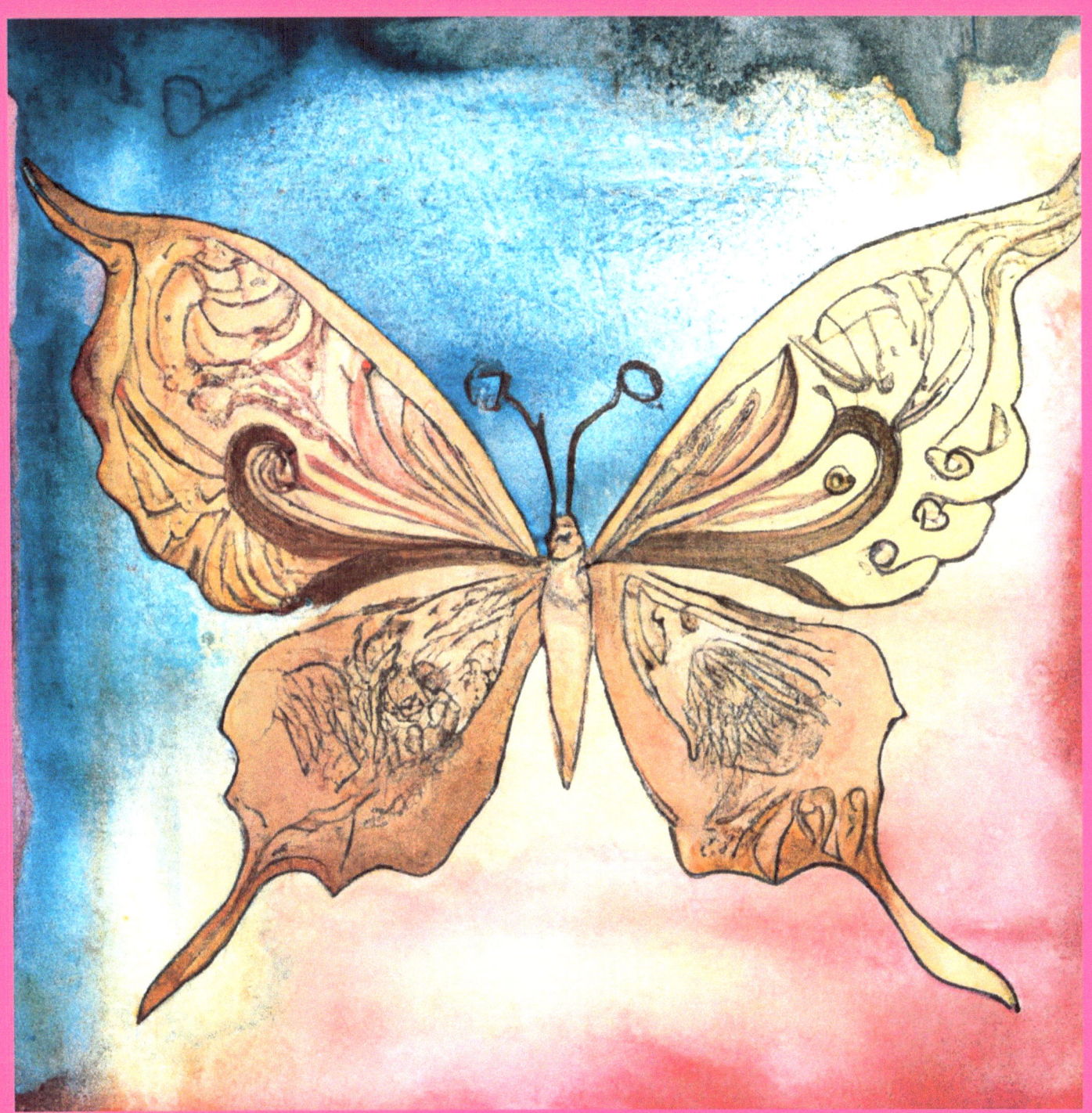

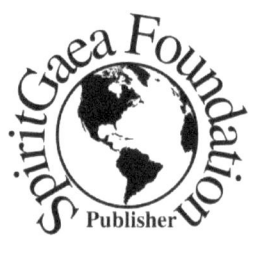

Author Artist

**Original Art
by Jeri Lee**

Copyright Jerilee.com
2022
All rights Reserved

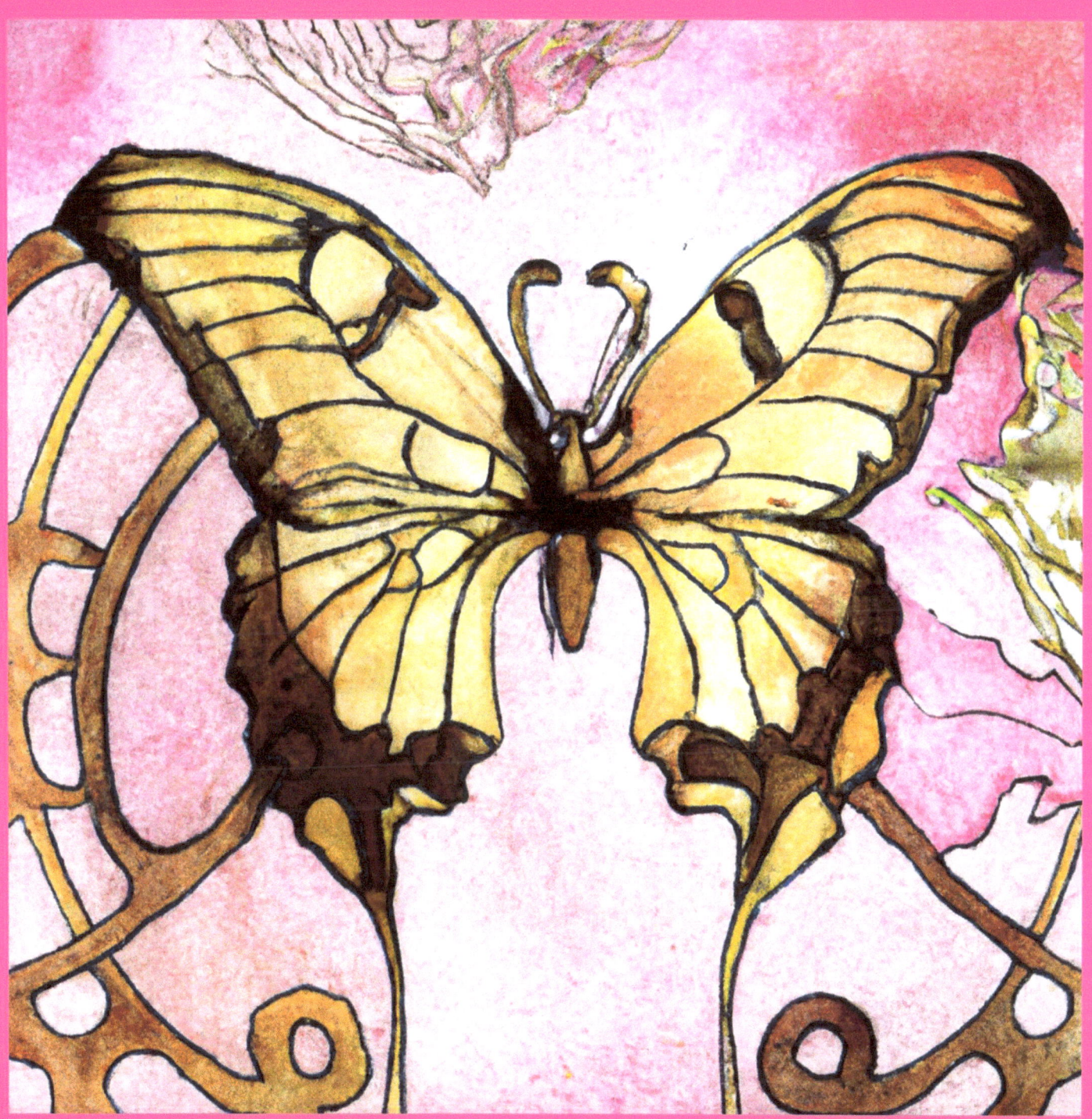

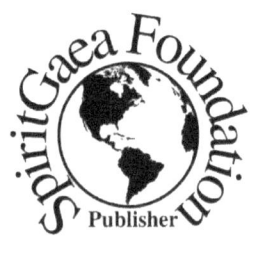

**Original Art
by Jeri Lee**

Copyright Jerilee.com
2022
All rights Reserved

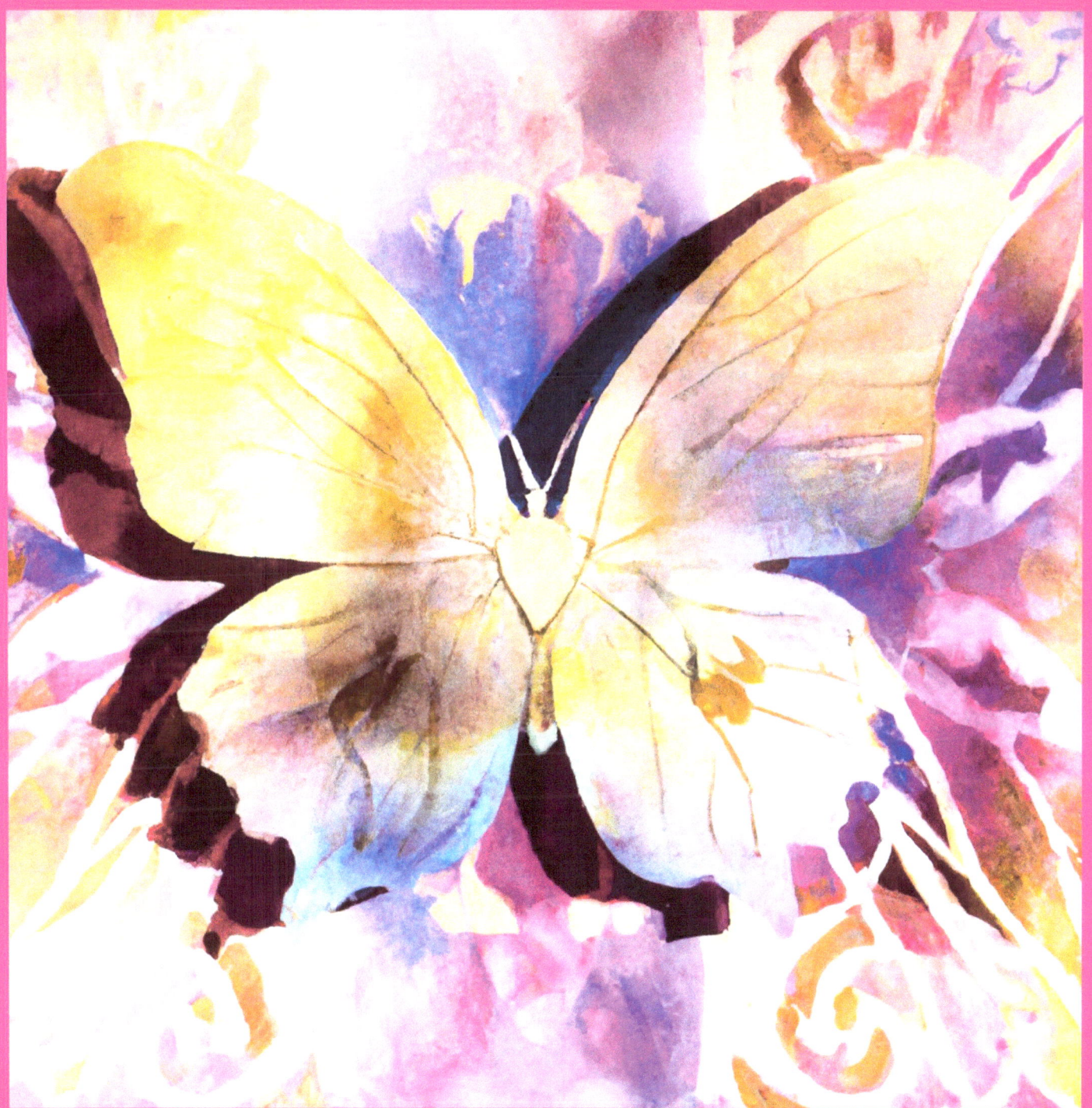

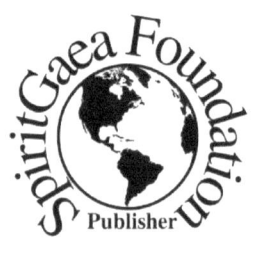

Author Artist

**Original Art
by Jeri Lee**

Copyright Jerilee.com
2022
All rights Reserved

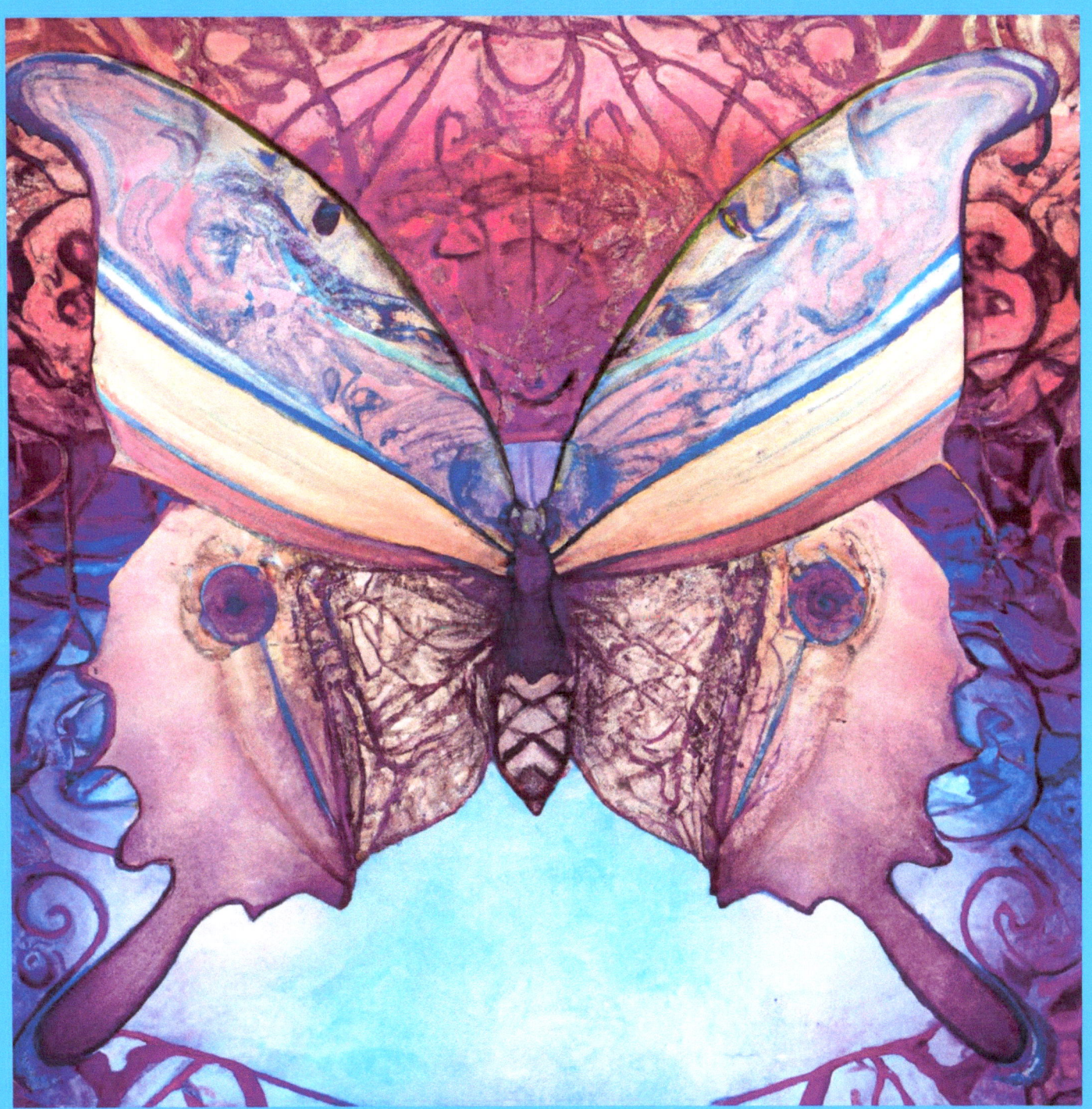

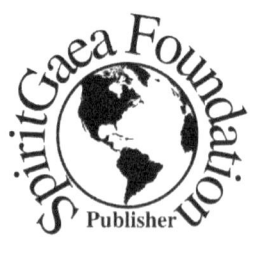

Author Artist

**Original Art
by Jeri Lee**

Copyright Jerilee.com
2022
All rights Reserved

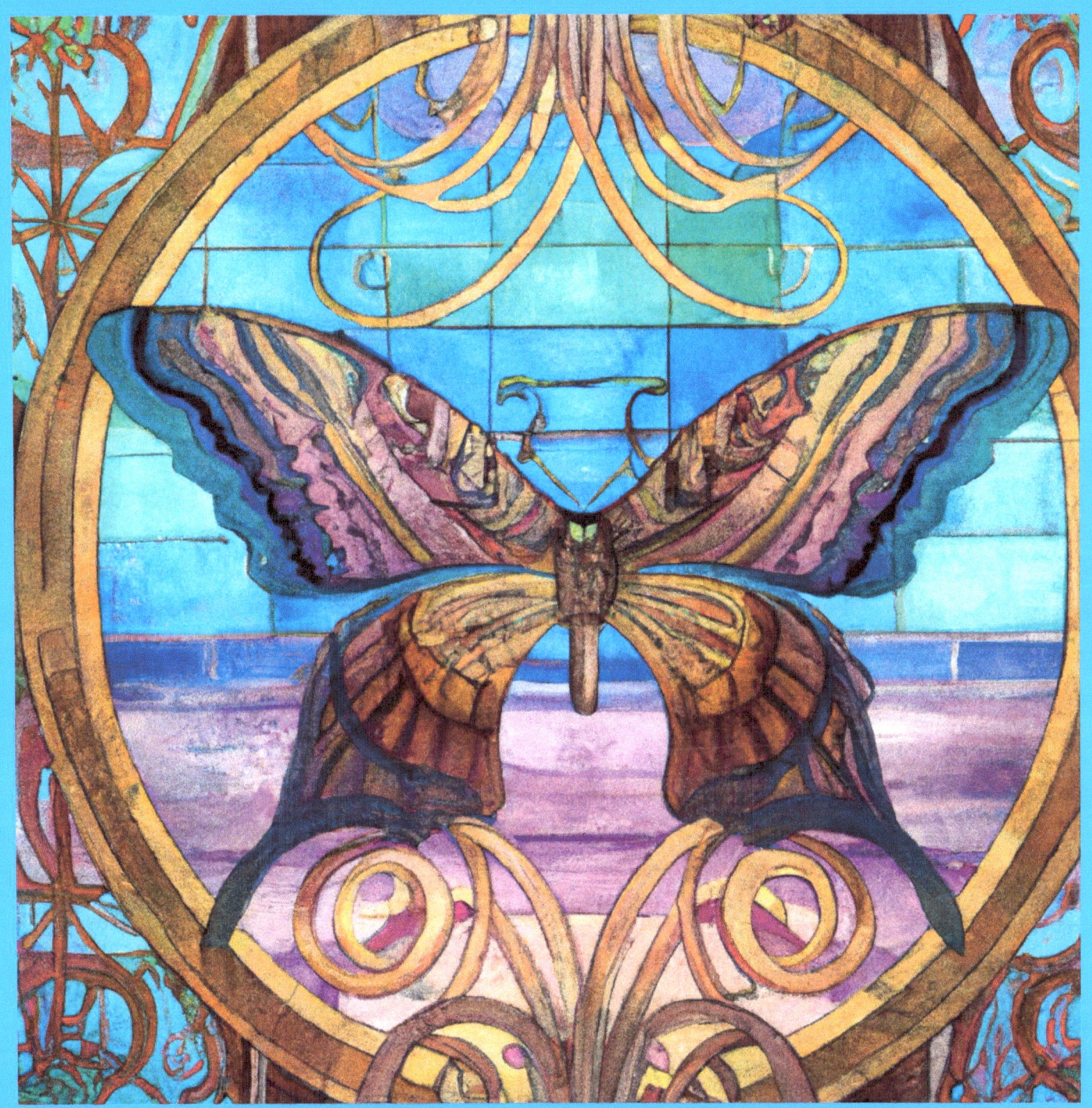

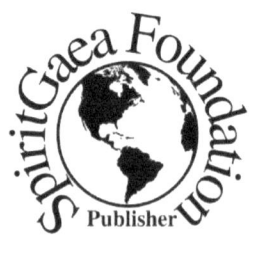

Author Artist

**Original Art
by Jeri Lee**

Copyright Jerilee.com
2022
All rights Reserved

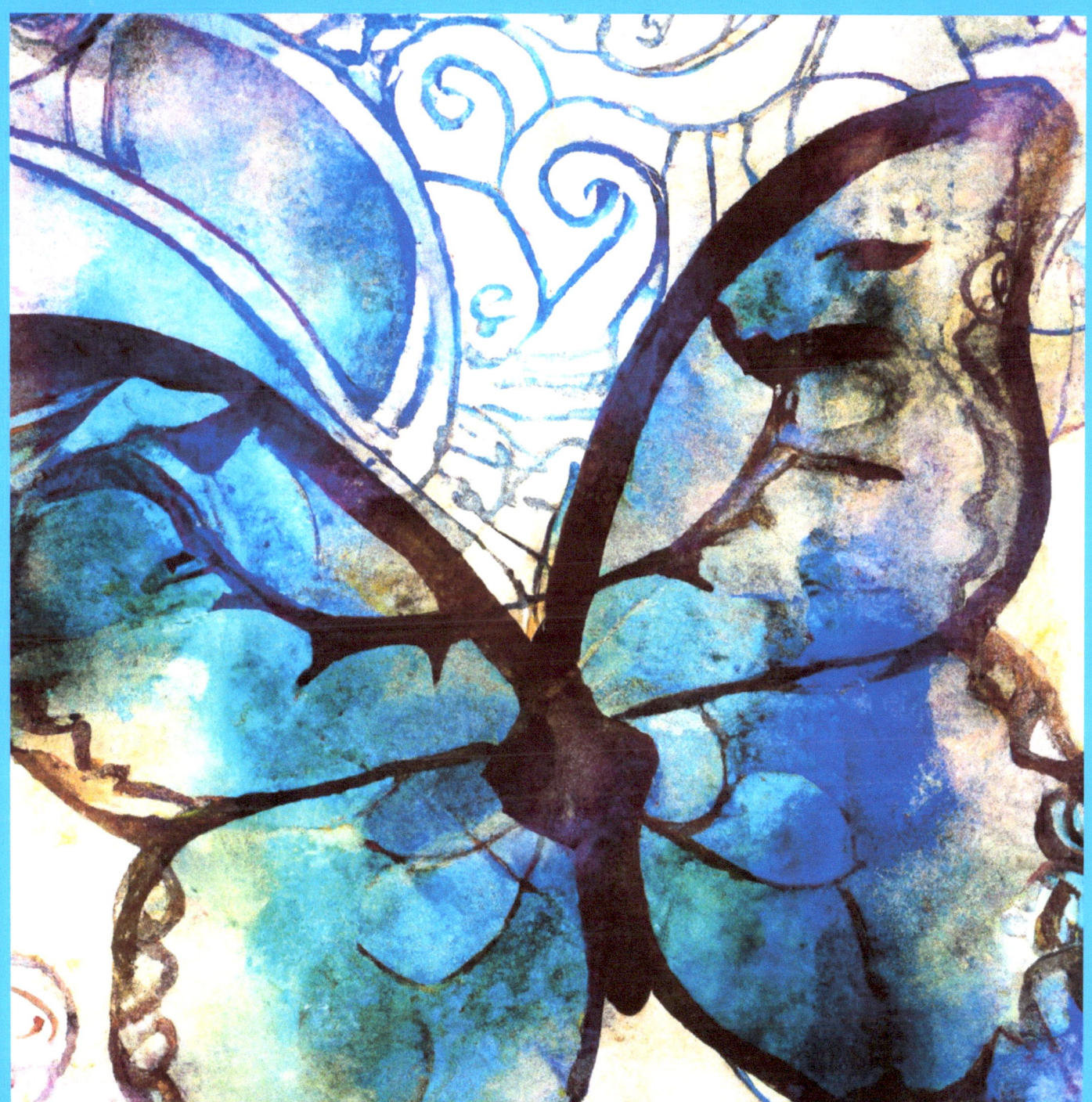

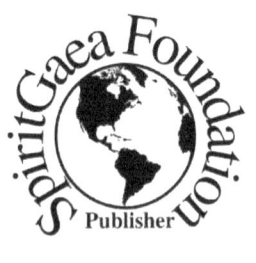

Author Artist

**Original Art
by Jeri Lee**

Copyright Jerilee.com
2022
All rights Reserved

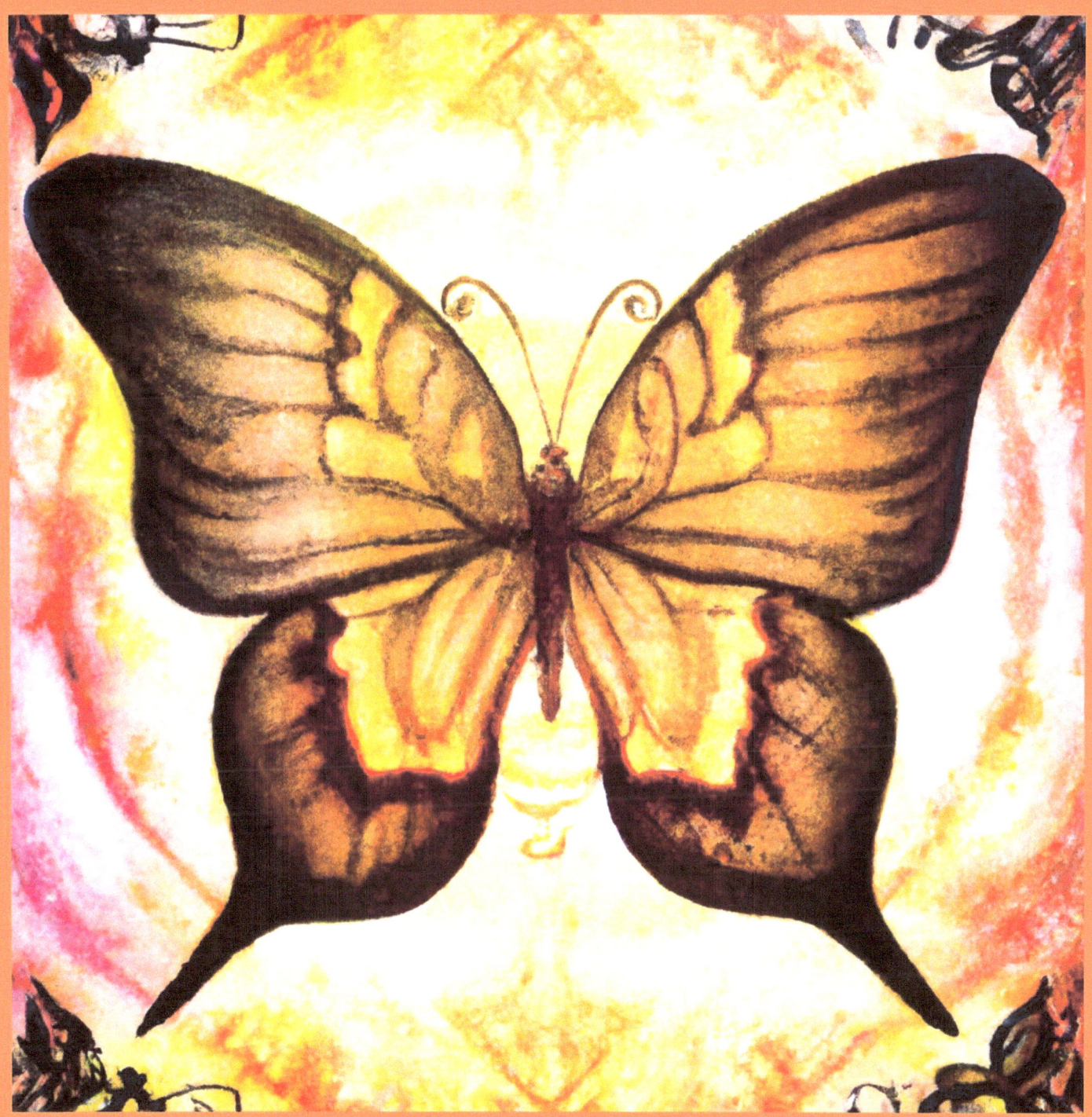

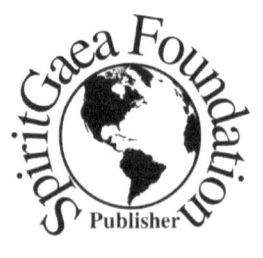

Author Artist

**Original Art
by Jeri Lee**

Copyright Jerilee.com
2022
All rights Reserved

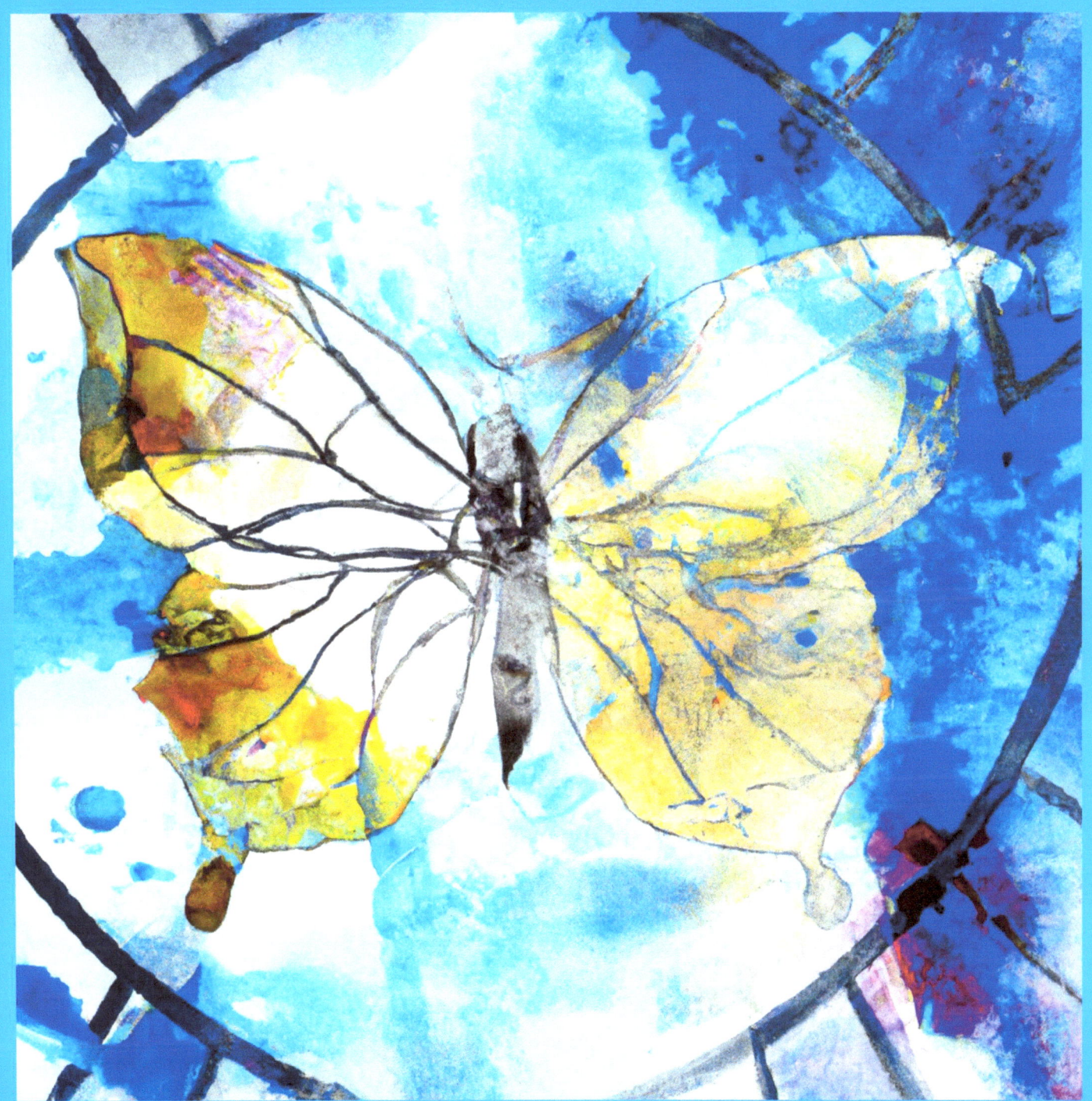

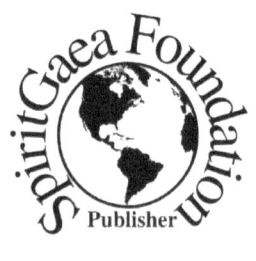

Author Artist

**Original Art
by Jeri Lee**

Copyright Jerilee.com
2022
All rights Reserved

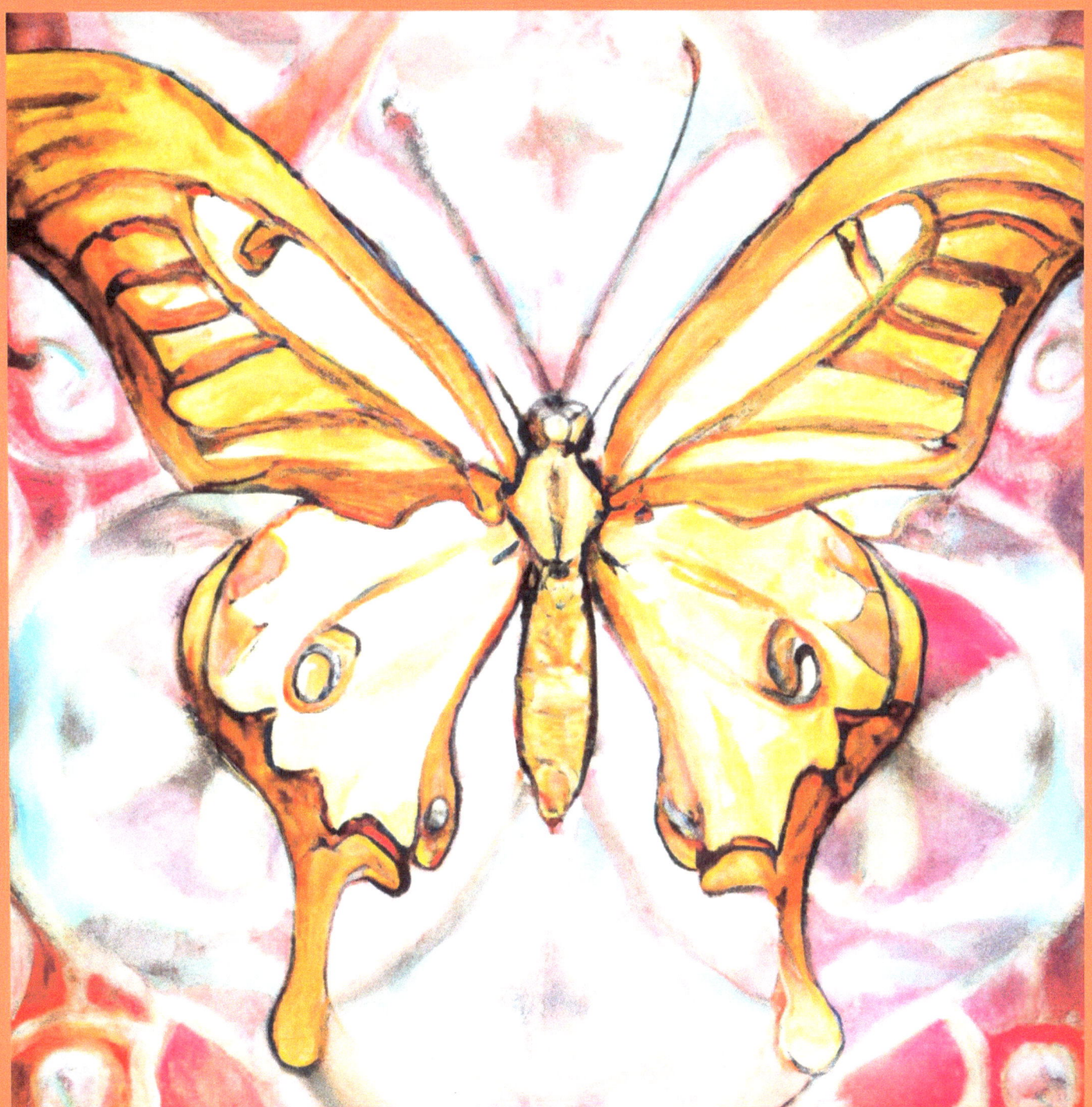

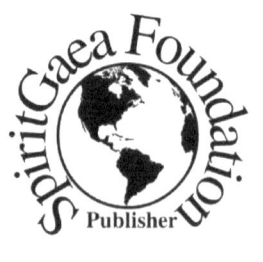

Author Artist

**Original Art
by Jeri Lee**

Copyright Jerilee.com
2022
All rights Reserved

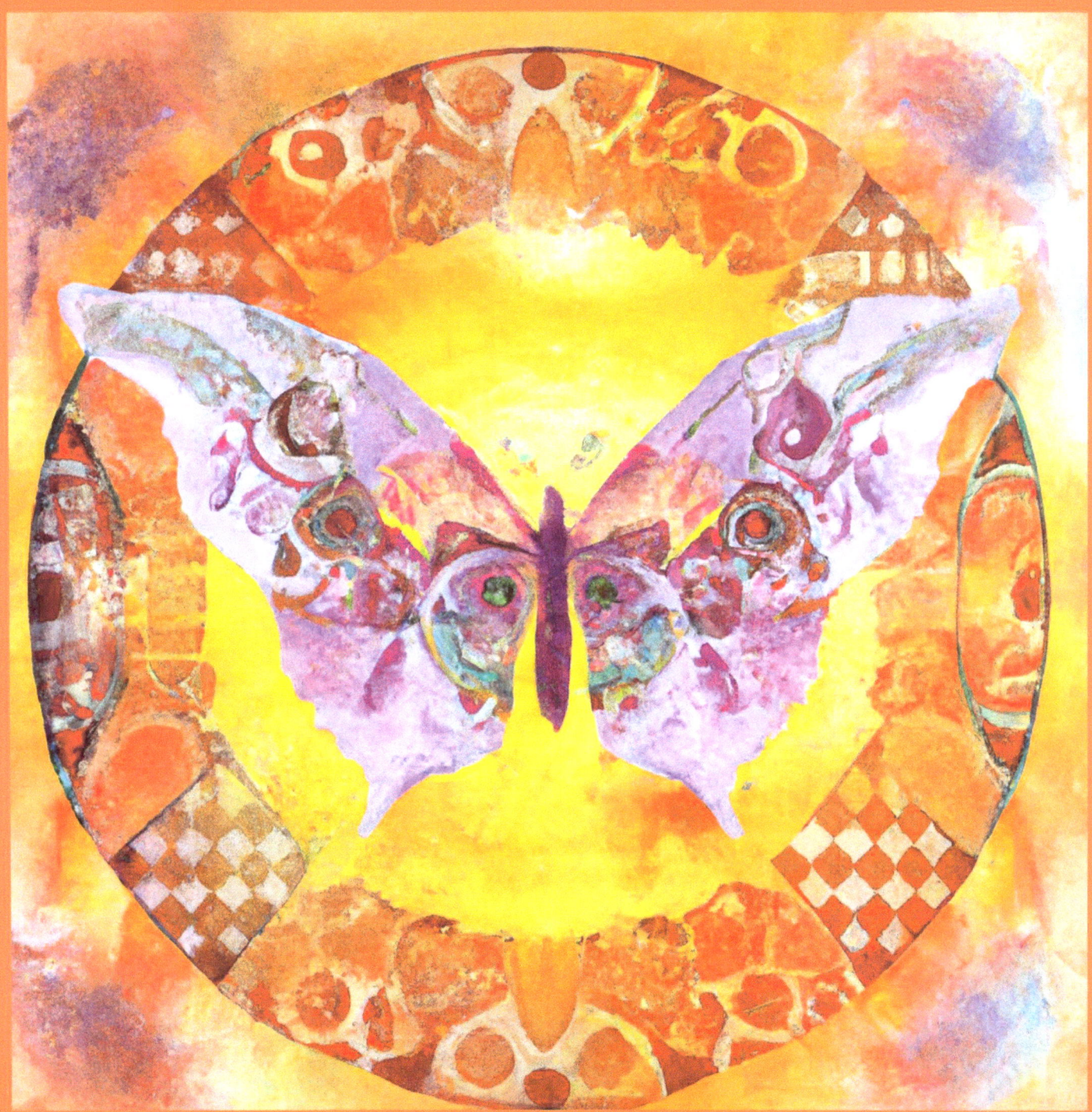

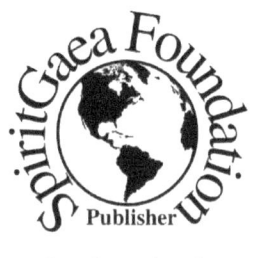

Author Artist

**Original Art
by Jeri Lee**

Copyright Jerilee.com
2022
All rights Reserved

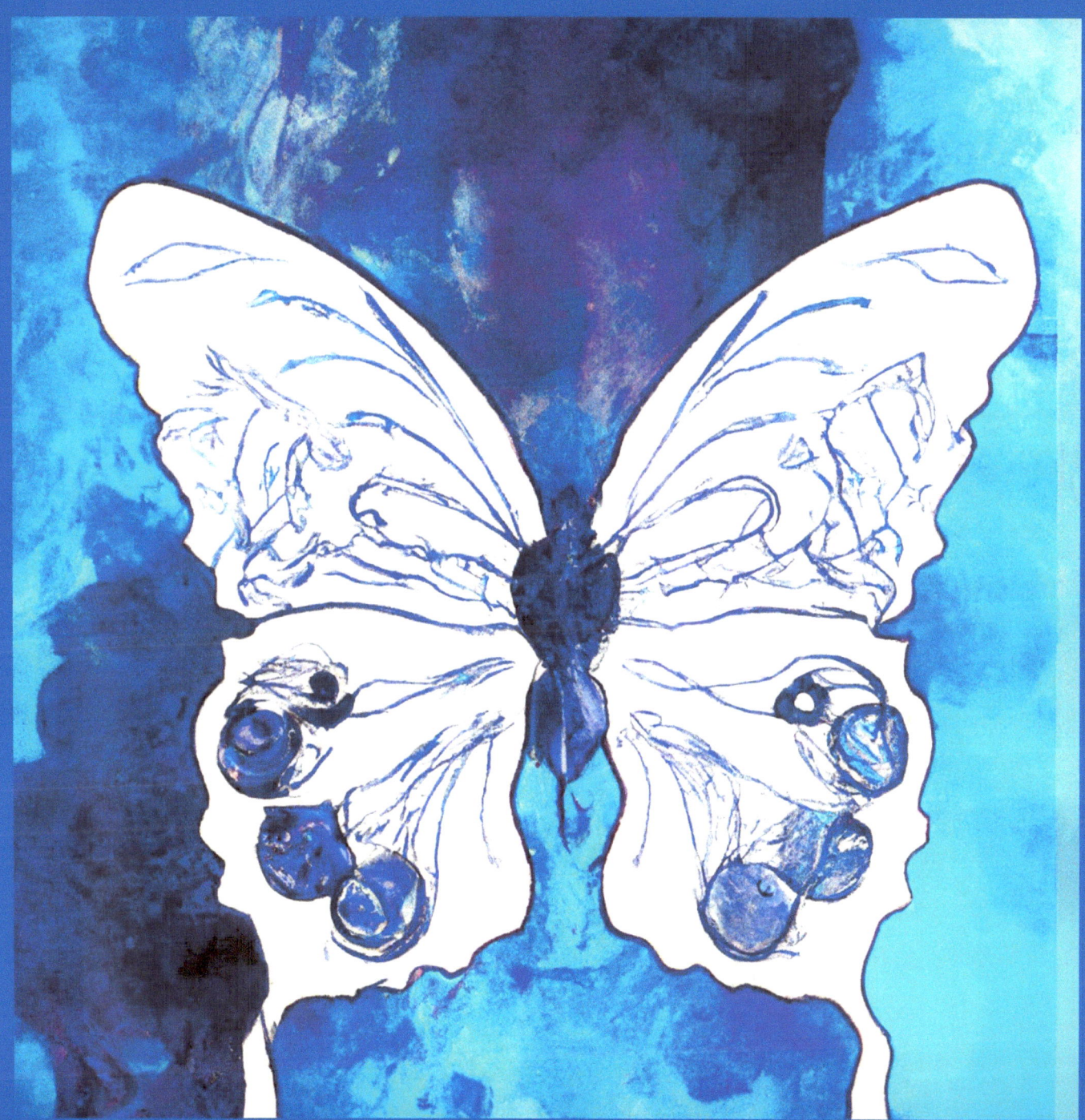

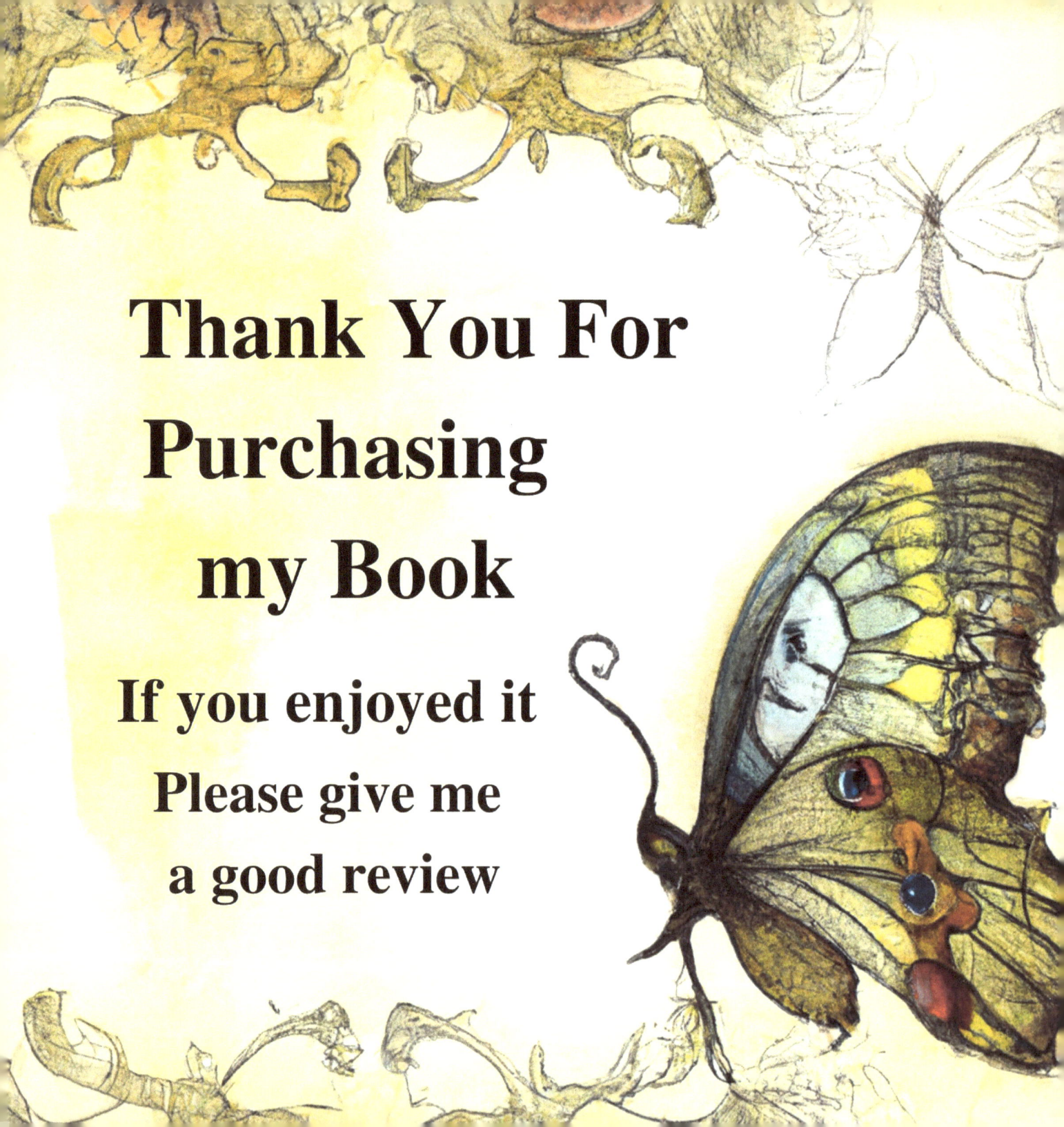

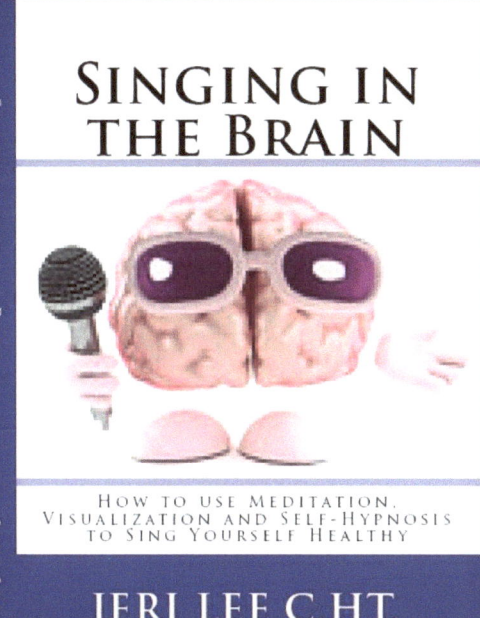

About the Artist-Author

I was born in 1939 with an overactive ambition that even death could not alter. I have died twice but refuse to stay dead. I wrote Singiiing in the brain as a self-help book to share what I do to stay alive even in my 80s. From early life, pushing a pen or a brush has been my way of life.

Singing in the Brain

By using Meditation, Visualization and Self-Hypnosis you can sing yourself healthy. You utilize your right brain functions when you sing. Your voice is your best friend and is your natural tranquilizer so stay happy and healthy by singing to yourself. This is the true story of Author Jeri Lee, showing how she developed this process. This is a do it yourself book on finding your fountain of youth

t

You Might enjoy one of my many coloring books, Most of which are designed with Adults in mind.

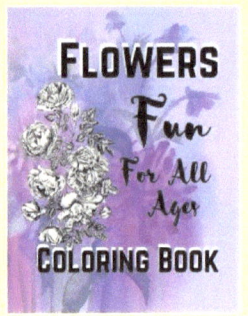
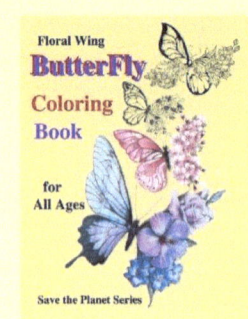
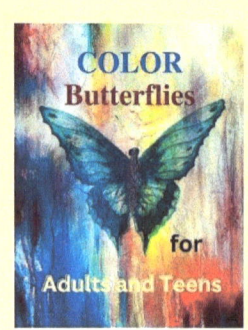

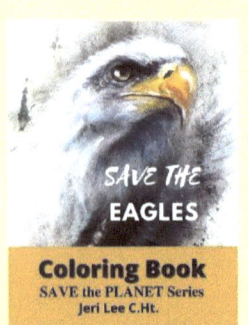
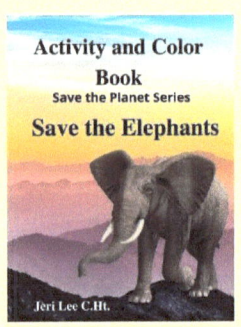
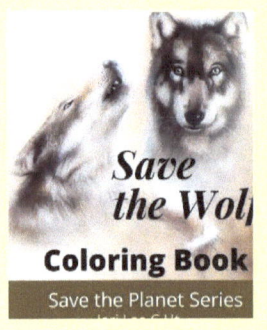
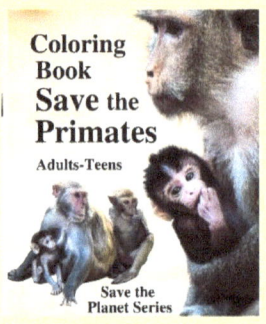
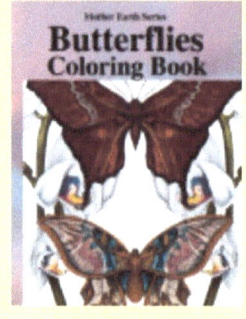

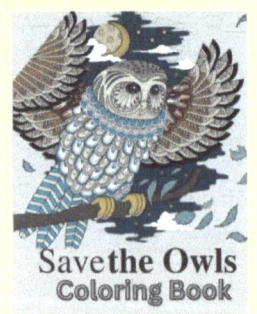
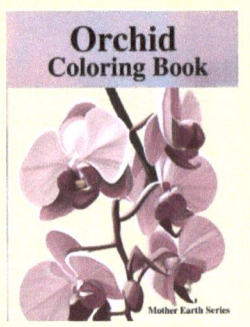
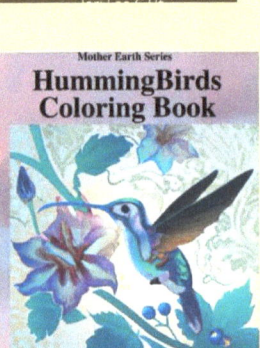
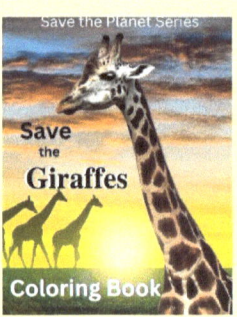
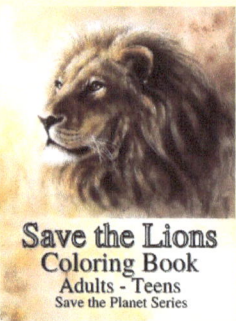

My Coloring books are 8.5 x 11 with 50 to 100 pages to color. They are focused on Save the Planet and pages can be view on my website. www,jerilee.com   purchases on Amazon.com

www.ingramcontent.com/pod-product-compliance
Lightning Source LLC
Chambersburg PA
CBHW051203220526
45473CB00003B/891